The P of Object Relations Therapy

A Series of Books Edited By
David E. Scharff and Jill Savege Scharff

THE
LIBRARY OF
OBJECT
RELATIONS

Object relations theories of human interaction and development provide an expanding, increasingly useful body of theory for the understanding of individual development and pathology, for generating theories of human interaction, and for offering new avenues of treatment. They apply across the realms of human experience from the internal world of the individual to the human community, and from the clinical situation to everyday life. They inform clinical technique in every format from individual psychoanalysis and psycho-therapy, through group therapy, to couple and family therapy.

The Library of Object Relations aims to introduce works that approach psychodynamic theory and therapy from an object relations point of view. It includes works from established and new writers who employ diverse aspects of British, American, and international object relations theory in helping individuals, families, couples, and groups. It features books that stress integration of psychoanalytic approaches with marital, family, and group therapy, as well as those centered on individual psychotherapy and psychoanalysis.

The Primer of Object Relations Therapy

by Jill Savege Scharff, M.D.,
and David E. Scharff, M.D.

JASON ARONSON INC.
Northvale, New Jersey
London

1997 Printing

Production Editor: Judith D. Cohen

This book was set in 11/14 point Times Roman.

The authors gratefully acknowledge permission to reprint revised or abbreviated material from the following sources:

> *Family Therapy Networker* for permission to use a revised edition of "Joining the Family: Countertransference Can Be the Therapist's Compass." *The Family Therapy Networker,* September/October, 1991. Copyright © 1991 by *The Family Therapy Networker.*

> Routledge and Kegan Paul for permission to reproduce the figure "The Endopsychic Situation" and the amended figure "Projective and Introjective Identification" from *The Sexual Relationship.* Copyright © 1982 by David E. Scharff.

Library of Congress Cataloging-in-Publication Data

Scharff, Jill Savege.
    Scharff Notes : a primer of object relations therapy / by Jill Savege Scharff and David E. Scharff.
      p. cm.
    Includes bibliographical references and index.
    ISBN 1-56821-774-9
    1. Object relations (Psychoanalysis) 2. Psychotherapy.
I. Scharff, David E., 1941-   II. Title.
    [DNLM: 1. Object Attachment. 2. Psychoanalytic Therapy. WM
460.5.02 S311s]
RC489.025S34 1992
616.89'14—dc20
DNLM/DLC
for Library of Congress   92-10495

Printed in the United States of America on acid-free paper. For information and catalog write to Jason Aronson Inc., 230 Livingston Street, Northvale, New Jersey 07647. Or visit our website: http://www.aronson.com

Dedicated to
Kate, Nell, Zoe, Xanthe,
and Daniel

Contents

PART II
OBJECT RELATIONS THEORY IN PRACTICE

PART III
APPLICATION AND INTEGRATION

PART IV
THE OBJECT RELATIONS THERAPIST:
FURTHER TRAINING AND GUIDED READING

LIST OF FIGURES

LIST OF TABLES

Preface

A s we traveled around the United States teaching seminars in object relations therapy, we recognized the need for a basic text. So we decided to write this primer on British object relations theory. We want to reach the undergraduate student who is learning the fundamentals of theory and therapy as well as the graduate student in psychology, social work, or marital and family therapy. We hope to interest first-year residents in psychiatry and interns in psychology, social work, marital and family therapy, and pastoral counseling. We think that the book will be useful for trainees in occupational therapy, art and other expressive therapies, and psychiatric nursing. And finally, we hope that the primer will be a compact and convenient resource text for the teachers of these various undergraduate, graduate, and postgraduate students, and for the experienced clinician who wants to integrate the unfamiliar perspective of object relations theory into an existing approach.

The primer stands alone or may prepare the reader for wider reading in object relations theory, including study of our more advanced texts: *Object Relations Family Therapy, Foundations of Object Relations Family Therapy, Object Relations Couple Therapy, Projective and Introjective Identification and the Use of the Therapist's Self, Refinding the Object and Reclaiming the Self* (Jason Aronson Inc. 1987, 1989, 1991, 1992, and 1992, respectively), and *The Sexual Relationship: an Object Relations View of Sex and the Family* (Routledge and Kegan Paul 1982).

Mental health professionals from remote parts of the country have no access to object relations theory other than through textbooks. When puzzled, they have no colleagues to turn to for help. Although they may have enjoyed our more complex books, they want simplification and clarification of some of the ideas and further discussion of how the concepts apply in their clinical situations. The content of this volume derives from these students' most frequently asked questions, together with our responses. Through our lecture, discussion, and dialogue format, we re-create the seminar for them and for you, in order to take you beyond the forbidding aspects of theory and technique and give you access to object relations theory and therapy as a sensible way of thinking and working that is easily understood and immediately applicable to clinical practice.

We would like to thank Debby Ziff and Jo Parker for typing the first draft at lightning speed. We are grateful to Pearl Green for taking care of our children and to Kate and Nell Scharff for entertaining them so that we had time to write. We thank Carolyn Gruber and Kathleen Gray who read our manuscript to assess its relevance to their psychotherapy curricula in local schools of social work.

We remain grateful to our supportive and enthusiastic publisher, Jason Aronson, who welcomed the idea of a primer and who authorized the Object Relations Seminars at which we had the teaching experience that led to this work. It was a pleasure working with our calm, attentive production editor, Judy Cohen, her editorial director, Muriel Jorgensen, and editorial assistant Cheryl Ballew, who handled promotion.

We have reinvented the identities of the subjects of our clinical descriptions so as to preserve a personal context for their universally observable dynamics without betraying their confidentiality. To those individuals, couples, and families, we give special thanks.

We gratefully acknowledge the intellectual stimulation and encouragement from mental health professionals at our seminars, where their questions continually provoked further thought and challenged us to be clear and concise. This book is for them and for you, mental health professionals and students who are curious about the object relations approach.

How To Use This Primer

I n the interest of readability, we do not break the flow to pause for references in the body of this text. When we use a concept or an author's name with which you may not be familiar, we cite it briefly in the chapter notes that follow each chapter. In Chapter 19, we offer a guide to further reading both for the beginner and for the advanced student of object relations theory. To satisfy our concern for attribution and accessibility to reference materials, we do give a complete reference section at the end of the book. The reference section is divided into eight categories to simplify the advancing student's search for more to read in a particular category of interest. The eight categories are: object relations theory of individual and group, application of object relations theory to couple and family therapy, countertransference, integration with other approaches from the analytic to the behavioral, integration with American interpersonalists and classical Freudian theory, self psychology, Freudian theory, and other relevant contributions.

With this design, you can read uninterruptedly and take in the material as a whole the first time through. You can skip the references altogether, look at them at the end of reading each chapter or not until you have finished the book. Those of you who want to track down sources will search for author and date in the chapter notes at the end of each chapter and then find the full annotation in the relevant category of the formal reference section at the end of the book. We hope that this primer format will bring object relations theory to you clearly and easily.

The primer may be used as the only text on object relations theory for the eclectic therapist. It serves as an introduction and guide to reading our more advanced texts. It also leads to wider recommended reading in object relations theory and therapy.

I

Overview of the Concepts of British Object Relations Theory

ONE

The Self and
Its Objects

WHAT IS BRITISH OBJECT
RELATIONS THEORY?

British object relations theory is a theory of the human personality developed from study of the therapist–patient relationship as it reflects the mother–infant dyad. The theory holds that the infant's experience in relationship with the mother is the primary determinant of personality formation and that the infant's need for attachment to the mother is the motivating factor in development of the infantile self. It is an amalgam of the work of British analysts Ronald Fairbairn, Donald Winnicott, Harry Guntrip, and Michael Balint, of the British Independent group, augmented by those of Melanie Klein and the Kleinian group. Although Independent and Kleinian theories are quite distinct

4

from each other, and differ in the ways that each diverges from Sigmund Freud's theory of the mind, they are similar in focusing on the importance of the infant's experience of the mothering relationship. The Independent group followed Freud's use of the psychosexual stages of development, but disagreed that the inevitable progression of these stages was based on the primacy of the instincts. They proposed instead that the need to be in relationship to a caregiver was the fundamental driving force and that the characteristic kinds of relatedness seen at various ages were determined by shifting dependent needs, not by instinctual loading of the erogenous bases. The Kleinians stayed true to Freud's view of the instincts and elaborated upon the death instinct, but they revised his psychosexual stage timetable. They described their ideas of how the infant uses unconscious fantasy to effect the release of tension from the instincts and how the processing of fantasy creates psychic structure. Both Independent group and Kleinian theorists developed theories of personality formation and psychic structure different from Freud's, and different from each other. Nevertheless, the theories can be integrated because of their commonality in focus on the first three years of life—in analytic theory referred to as the preoedipal period of development—and their emphasis on the experience of the mother–infant relationship as the major component of psychic structure formation.

WHAT ARE OBJECT RELATIONS?

Object relations is an inclusive technical term that spans the intrapsychic and interpersonal dimensions. It refers to the system of in-built parts of the personality in relation to each other inside the self. These are expressed in the arena of current relationships by which the original intrapsychic constructions of object relations are further modified. Internal objects and other parts of the self are reciprocal with outer objects so that, in any relationship, the personalities are mutually influenced by each other. Our external relationships are in interaction with our internal psychic structures.

WHAT IS AN INTERNAL OBJECT?

An internal object is a piece of psychic structure that formed from the person's experience with the important caretaking person in earlier life, captured in the personality as the trace of that earlier relationship. Not a memory, nor a representation, it is a part of the self's being.

HOW IS THE INTERNAL OBJECT DIFFERENT FROM THE EXTERNAL OBJECT?

The external object refers to the significant other with whom the person is in relationship. It might refer to the early significant other or the present significant other. It bears a relationship to the internal object in that the internal object is based on the experience with the original external object and is expressed in the present choice of an external object. The internal object is also modified by its relationship with the present external object.

WHAT ARE THE FACTORS THAT KEEP THE INTERNAL OBJECT FROM BEING MERELY A DIRECT, INTERNAL RECORDING OF EXPERIENCE WITH THE EARLY EXTERNAL OBJECT?

There are several factors. During the early relationship to the mother, the baby has a limited capacity to understand what the mother is feeling or expressing or to separate this from what the baby feels. The baby's limited cognitive capacity distorts the view of the mother, so that already the internal object does not accurately reflect the external object. Later on, as the baby grows and develops, new issues at the forefront of development change what the baby thinks is happening with the external object. So it creates a contemporary version of the internal object to internalize. For instance, when the child is at a point where autonomy and control are at the leading edge of development, the child's capacity to hold on to and let go of the external object reshapes the internal object's organization. In summary, previous experience with the external object at all stages of development is cumulatively internalized. When child, adolescent, and adult meet new people, they will expect the new relationships to be like those they have known. Even if they are not really like that, the new figures may be experienced as though they were, in order to reaffirm that new experience is familiar and will not create a demand for change in the internal object relationships. Pressure from healthy, new external objects to maintain their own integrity reverses this trend. Then, new relationships can afford both partners the opportunity for further modification of their internal object worlds.

DOES THE HUMAN PERSONALITY CONSIST ONLY OF A COLLECTION OF OBJECTS?

No. Objects are only part of the personality. The child is born with its own potential personality. At birth, there is a self ready and pre-wired to relate to the external objects that the infant will find in the environment. In relation to these external objects, the self then grows and develops and builds upon its experience with the objects to create psychic structure.

WHAT IS THE SELF?

The self refers to the total personality growing through the life cycle. At first it is a pristine, unformed self, gradually becoming enriched by experience with the objects. According to infant researcher Daniel Stern, the baby is organized from the beginning to acquire experience in order to build a personality and a sense of self. The self comprises: (1) the old-fashioned concept of the ego as an executive mechanism that modulates self-control through its control of motility, sphincters, and affect states, and that mediates relations with the outside world, (2) the internal objects, and (3) objects and parts of the ego bound together by the affects (feelings) appropriate to the child's experiences of these object relationships.

We've used the term *self* to refer to the combination of ego and internal objects in a unique, dynamic relation that comprises the character and gives a sense of personal identity that endures and remains relatively constant over time.

WHAT IS THE RELATIONSHIP BETWEEN SELF AND OBJECT?

The self is the unique psychic organization that creates a person's identity. The external object is what the whole self relates to when it interacts with another person. The internal object is one of the substructures of the self. Also inside the self are various other internal objects and parts of the ego that correspond to them. The ego and its parts moderate operations and feelings that are identified with the self, organized in subcategories of the ego. These broad subcategories relate to corresponding internal objects. These categories of the self and their relevant objects are bound together by the emotion or affect that characterizes the object relationship. Different kinds of internal object relationships arise during different affect states.

CAN YOU DEFINE AN INTERNAL OBJECT RELATIONSHIP?

Internal object relationship is a term for the relationship between part of the ego and its object bound together by the feelings that were experienced by the ego in relation to that object. The internal object relationship becomes an enduring, but potentially modifiable, part of the self that may remain in consciousness or may need to be pushed out of consciousness if it provokes intolerable anxiety.

We now have a view of the self as consisting of conscious and unconscious parts. Object relations theorists hold that the unconscious is part of the ego, in contrast to Freud, who described the unconscious as separate from the ego, located in a part of the personality that he called the "id"—a seething mass of impulses seeking discharge and governed by irrational thinking processes.

HOW DOES THE INTERNAL OBJECT RELATIONSHIP FORM IF THE MOTHER IS NOT RAISING THE CHILD?

At their time of writing, the theorists were thinking of the influence on the child of mothering by the actual mother, the woman who had borne the child or who had undertaken to raise the child. Fairbairn and Winnicott noticed the reality of the holding and handling of the child, but also noted the influence of the mother's personality on the mother–infant relationship, whereas Klein was more concerned with the infant's fantasies about the relationship. All of them underemphasized the father's contribution to the child's experience, except as the mother's partner.

Nowadays, with fathers taking a more active part in the

raising of their children and mothers working outside the home, we use the term *mother* to refer to the person who is centrally responsible for the daily care of the child. This person might be the actual mother (biological or adoptive), the father, an older sibling, the family housekeeper, or, more likely, a combination of them. The impact of family dynamics on the individual development of the older child has been described by Roger Shapiro and John Zinner. We need more studies of the effect that sharing of the mothering function has on the infant's development to be more precise about its impact on personality, but for now we can say that the infant integrates experience with multiple external objects to arrive at composite internal objects. All of these significant people are in relationship to each other. The relationship between these external objects affects the integration of composite internal objects and their internal dynamic relation.

WHY WOULD IT NOT BE BETTER TO CALL THE THEORY "SUBJECT RELATIONS THEORY"?

Some people find the term *object relations theory* rather cold and impersonal. They might feel happier calling it *subject relations theory*. We stick to Fairbairn's original "object relations" terminology, which was developed from its base in Freud's theory. Freud used the word *object* to refer to the target that the drives aimed at and looked to for gratification in the person of the caretaker. In his view, the object of the drives was not personal, because the drives were an impersonal force seeking discharge.

For us, however, the object is not an impersonal matter. Our view stems from Fairbairn's original assertion that the need for a relationship is primary (not the need for instinctual tension release) and that the person in whose care the child is growing is vitally important as an object of attachment (not of drive gratification).

WHY NOT CALL THIS APPROACH "PERSONAL RELATIONS THEORY"?

This does sound more human, but it does not do justice to the history of the development of the ideas, and it colloquializes what is really a technical matter. We reserve the term *object relations theory* precisely to highlight the technical aspects of the theory and its clinical application.

NOTES

For an excellent, concise overview of the contributions of Fairbairn (1944, 1952, 1954, 1958, 1963), Winnicott (1951, 1956, 1958, 1964, 1965, 1971), Guntrip (1961, 1969, 1986) and Balint (1968), we suggest the review article, "The British Object Relations Theorists: Balint, Winnicott, Fairbairn, Guntrip" (Sutherland 1980). For an easy approach to the theories of Klein (1935, 1946, 1948, 1952, 1955, 1957, 1975), see Segal (1964) and Klein and Riviere (1967). The work of Freud (1895, 1900, 1901, 1905, 1910a, 1910b, 1911, 1912, 1915a, 1915b, 1915c, 1917a, 1917b, 1917c, 1920, 1921, 1923, 1924, 1930, 1933) is summarized for the beginner in Freud's introductory lectures on psychoanalysis (Freud 1910a) and for the advanced reader in his final published paper (Freud 1940), written at the age of 82. The contribution of infant research to the development of the self is found in Stern (1985). Papers by Shapiro (1979) and Zinner (1989) and Zinner and Shapiro (1972) are reprinted in *Foundations of Object Relations Family Therapy* (Scharff 1989).

TWO

Basic Freudian Concepts

WHAT ARE FREUD'S BASIC CONCEPTS?

Before we look at Fairbairn's scheme of the endopsychic structure of internal object relations in Chapter 3, we will review Freud's topographic and structural theories and his basic psychoanalytic concepts of (1) the unconscious, (2) the ego, the id, and superego, and (3) resistance and defense.

The topographic theory

Freud's most outstanding contribution was to show that human behavior is determined by factors outside conscious awareness.

From his study of associations to dreams and slips of the tongue, he concluded that some of a person's feelings and ideas could be separated off from the conscious thought in response to trauma in infancy. Such trauma might include a frightening event, a childhood seduction, a hospitalization, loss of a parent, and so on. The working of the unconscious was not governed by logic and reason, but by primitive, impulse-ridden thinking called *primary process.* Freud's idea of analysis was to trace the patient's associations to the manifest content of dreams and to slips of the tongue in order to reestablish the forgotten connections. In this way, he made the unconscious conscious, subjected it to the conscious form of thinking called *secondary process* governed by rules of reason, and so relieved the infantile neurosis. Freud originally described the mind as being divided into conscious, preconscious, and unconscious areas. This first tripartite theory is known as the topographical theory.

Structural theory

Many years later, Freud postulated another tripartite theory of the mind. In this theory he ascribed a structure to the unconscious. He called this the *id,* envisioned as a seething cauldron of aggressive and sexual drives. To mediate between the unruly id and the demands of external reality, the *ego* emerges out of the mess of the id. The ego is conceived as a structure mainly (though not entirely) associated with preconscious and conscious functioning. The ego comprises (1) the set of executive functions or mechanisms that mediate between the id and the outer world and (2) the set of accumulated identifications with the lost objects of the drives, all of which culminate in a personal identity. After the resolution of the oedipal period of development when the child gives up the wish to possess one parent and kill the rival, the third structure, called the *superego,* develops, based on selective identifications with the forbidding, critical qualities of the parents and reaction formations against these. The superego has both conscious and unconscious elements and guides the child toward moral responsibility. The topographic and structural theories cannot be superimposed exactly upon each other, but co-exist as useful ways of viewing the mind.

The theory of psychosexual development

Freud held that the human infant is motivated by two opposing instincts. At first, Freud saw these as the *sexual instinct* (also called *libido*), for getting on with life and enjoying sexual pleasure, and the *self-preservative instinct,* for repressing the sexual instinct in order to face reality. Later, he ascribed opposition to the sexual instinct in terms of the *death instinct,* of which the manifestations were harder for him to see but which he thought were diverted into the external world in the form of destructiveness and aggressiveness. These instincts, or *drives* as they are now more commonly called, have the *aim* of gratification by the *object* that they fall upon. Their *source* is the pool of instincts, impulses, or drives seething untamed in the unconscious part of the mind that Freud called the *id*. These instincts have to be tamed in order not to lose the love object. The infant takes inside successive versions of the love object that have to be given up at each stage of development, and out of these introjections are formed the child's *ego* (the conscious, executive part of the self) and *superego* (the critical, forbidding, guiding part of the self, based on the selective internalization of the parental functioning). Freud's case histories make it clear that he was well aware of the mother's holding and handling of her infant, but in the formulation of his theories he underemphasized the quality of the relationship. Instead, he focused on the structure and function of the child's mind in relative isolation and developed for this task a model of the mind based on science. The organism seeks (1) discharge of instinctual tension, (2) repetition of tension-reducing behavior so as to return to a state of *homeostasis,* or (3) *narcissistic* retreat into the self, where needs either do not disturb or their satisfaction can be imagined as vividly as if it were occurring.

The psychosexual stages of development

The instincts go through a series of *psychosexual stages of development* that unfold in a predetermined, universal sequence.

Preoedipal development

At first predominantly *oral* in nature, the instincts propel the infant to suck both for survival through being fed and for pleasurable, libidinal gratification, and later to bite and spit as a way of releasing aggression. When the mouth gives way to the *anus* as the dominant *erogenous zone,* the child gains pleasure from the feces and from the control the anus can exert over holding on to or letting go of them. In the *phallic* stage of development, the child is now aware of and seeks genital sensations, often confused with the urethral sensations of urination. As always, the drives seek objects to gratify their expressions. Naturally, the mother is training her child to gain control over these impulses, and so she becomes forbidding as well as gratifying of her child's wishes. Aware of differences in the genitalia between the sexes, the female child imagines that the more obvious penis affords the boy greater pleasure than she enjoys. This is a source of unhappiness and sometimes shame and poor self-esteem. The sequence now moves on to the *oedipal phase.*

Oedipal development

The little girl develops the fantasy of getting a penis for herself: the best and biggest is the one that she seeks, namely, her father's. The child does not want to admit that this is her mother's territory and imagines that she may have to get rid of her Mommy so as to have her Daddy, and any babies that he might give her, all to herself. The girl is then afraid of an angry mother who will kill her or her unborn babies. The boy notices that his mother is interested in his father and assumes that her interest has to do with her wish for his penis. Size comparisons notwithstanding, the boy hopes that his mother will find his penis more attractive than her husband's. If not, the boy imagines, he may have to kill his rival, the father, who, if he should find this out, might angrily retaliate by killing the boy (or at least he might cut off his penis to punish him for wanting his mother). Freud called the boy's fear of retaliation *castration anxiety.* The girl was thought to have a *castration complex,* in other words to be upset that she had already been castrated.

Freud thought that the girl's feminine identity formed as a result of her castration complex, namely, her sense of inferiority at not having a valued penis like a boy. His view of feminine identity as a deficit state has been successfully challenged by observational infant research, feminist psychology, and child analysis. We now know that girls have as strong a sense of sexual identity as do boys, long before the phallic period of development. Boys and girls alike envy each other's different sexual characteristics. Excessive signs of castration complex and penis envy in the girl occur when possessing a penis is imagined to make up for an inner sense of deficit or loneliness. Envy of the procreative power of the female body leaves the boy feeling inadequate. One defense against this is to devalue women and aggrandize phallic competence — which tends to drive the penis envy of women and so divert attention from the womb envy of men.

In both sexes, images of the forbidding parents are internalized as a part of the mind called the *superego,* which operates as a conscience and matures in its capacity for maintaining altruistic and moral values. Capable now of more complex thinking, the child realizes that there is no way of having everything and gives up forbidden sexual and murderous wishes to possess one parent and kill the other in favor of being the child of two parents who are together. The Oedipus complex is more or less resolved and the child moves on into the latency stage, where ego and superego defenses against regression are strengthened and issues of autonomy and skill-building come to the fore. If unable to master the challenges of a particular developmental stage, a child may become *fixated* there or even *regress* to an earlier developmental stage inappropriate to chronological age.

The nature of the *resolution of the Oedipus complex* determines the character structure, by 7 years of age, with one qualifier: the Oedipus constellation comes up for reworking during the sexually energized phase of adolescence. Its state of resolution by that time determines the ego's degree of disengagement from the old incestuous objects, which, in turn, determines how free the young person is to develop age-appropriate, sexually experimental love relationships with peers. The mate who is eventually selected will offer attraction and passionate attachment powerful enough to defeat the tie to the old objects and yet similar enough to inherit the transference to them.

Based in object relations theory, our ideas about the organizational boundaries of the unconscious differ from those of Freud. Nevertheless, we continue to view his concepts of unconscious motivation and unconscious organization as basic to any psychodynamic approach. Similarly, although we disagree with Freud's view of the instinctual basis of psychosexual development in which the sexual instinct cathects the erogenous zones in a preset sequence that then determines psychosexual development, we do find that the sequence occurs as Freud described it and that the child uses the oral, anal, urethral, phallic, and eventually genital routes for the experience of arousal and discharge of sexual and aggressive feeling. But we think that these feelings originate within the relationship to the caretaker as it evolves through the various stages of child-rearing, from the nursing, lap-baby stage, the toilet-training toddler stage, to the nursery-schooler who must separate from the mother and explore the wider world of friendships and sexual difference.

As Erik Erikson pointed out, when he reviewed the eight stages of man, there is a dilemma to be solved at each stage. At the oral stage, the task is to establish trust and find a balance between taking in and putting out. At the anal stage we are concerned with holding on and letting go of our parent as well as of our body products. At the phallic-urethral stage we want to be admired more than our rivals or else we feel ashamed and sometimes defective. At the genital level we are ready to give and receive love in a faithful, free way, no longer bound by a rivalrous obsession to possess the opposite-sex parent. Fairbairn regarded the stages of psychosexual development as reflecting the child's use of techniques of relating appropriate to the caretaker's attempts to train the dependent child.

According to Freud, the oedipal child wants to possess the opposite-sex parent and kill the rival to secure this goal. Fairbairn thought that the conflicts of the oedipal phase represented the child's attempt to simplify the following problem: In the preoedipal stage, the child had two ambivalently held relationships, one with mother and the other with father, each of them contributing elements to both the internal exciting and rejecting object relationships. In the oedipal phase, the child attempts to solve the ambivalence by making the relationship with one parent attractive and the other rejecting, at first possibly selecting the same-sex parent for the positive relationship, but at the height of the oedipal phase the attractive relationship is usually with the opposite-sex parent.

CAN YOU SAY MORE ABOUT THE ID?

In Freudian theory, the id comprises the sexual and aggressive instincts bursting to express themselves and find gratification. The organism wants to discharge the energy from these drives so that it can return to a state of non-excitation. The id is organized by primary process, a disorganized, primitive way of connecting ideas in a chaotic matrix. In the unconscious, troublesome thoughts and feelings get separated from the impulses in which they originated, and might then connect through primary process with some unrelated thought. Freud invented free association, a technique of saying whatever comes to mind — even if the thoughts do not seem to follow naturally — to retrace these random connections and so derive meaning from apparent non-sequiturs that could not be arrived at by formal inquiry.

How Is the Ego Different from the Id?

Freud wrote that the ego is organized according to secondary process thinking characterized by logic and reason rather than by unmitigated feelings and impulses under the pressure of instinctual tension. Secondary process is better suited to carrying out the executive functions of the ego, such as managing affect states, integrating whole object experience, identifying with object qualities, tolerating ambivalence, and relating to the outer world.

Why Do We Care About Conscious and Unconscious Levels of Organization?

They are useful clinically, as we conceptualize the treatment process. The task of treatment is to analyze the chaotic and confusing signals from the unconscious so as to free the ego for dealing with reality. Freud said simply that where id had been, ego would be. In other words, we work toward substituting conscious and more rational understanding for previously irrational behavior stemming from the primary process of the unconscious. Freud said that the goal of treatment is to make the unconscious conscious.

What Are Resistance and Defense?

Freud described resistance as a function of the patient's unconscious organization which tends to prevent unconscious things from becoming conscious. It goes against the patient's conscious wish to cooperate and get better, and it operates against the therapeutic effort and often against the person of the therapist. Much later, Sigmund Freud and his daughter Anna Freud described the personality as consisting of many defenses that are ego mechanisms for structuring and controlling unconscious impulses. Today we think of defense as an intrinsic part of character structure. Patterns of defense occur not so much to keep unconscious forces at bay as to structure the expression of deep-seated needs, affects, and conflicts, while protecting the vulnerabilities of the individual. All of this we now think of as happening within the context of the individual's need for primary relationships. Thus, defenses such as projection, denial, displacement, sublimation, reversal of affect, and reaction formation can all be seen as ways of structuring relationships.

NOTES

Freud's psychoanalytic theories appear in the *Standard Edition* of his work as follows:
> Topographic theory, the unconscious, primary process, the preconscious, consciousness, secondary process (1915c).
> Repression (1915a, 1915c)
> Structural theory, ego, id and superego (1923).
> Identification (1917a, 1923).
> Dream theory (1900).
> Slips of the tongue or parapraxes (1901).
> The sexual instinct, the self-preservative instinct, psychosexual stages of development (1905).
> The death instinct (1920, 1930).
> The Oedipus complex and its resolution (1910a, 1910b, 1924).
> Resistance, repression (1917c).
> Defense (1895).

For elaboration on the mechanisms of defense, see A. Freud (1946).

For the first extension of Freud's theory to a relational context, see Erikson (1950).

THREE

Endopsychic Structure

Fairbairn described three main categories of internal object relationship, one in the conscious part of the self and the other two repressed in the unconscious:

(1) the *ideal object relationship* (in the conscious part of the self), (2) the *exciting object relationship* (in the unconscious part of the self), and (3) the *rejecting object relationship* (in the unconscious part of the self). Fairbairn's model of psychic organization is summarized in Figure 3–1.

HOW DID THESE REPRESSED OBJECT RELATIONSHIPS DEVELOP?

Sorting and ordering of the internal psychological organization occur through the mechanism of splitting paired with repression. Fairbairn thought that the infant found even the good mother to

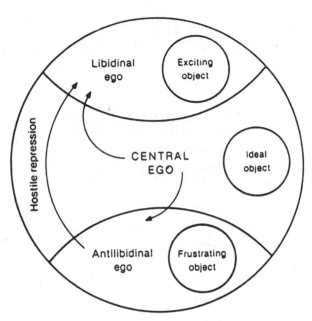

FIG. 3–1. The endopsychic situation.· Reprinted from *The Sexual Relationship: An Object Relations View of Sex and the Family,* courtesy of Routledge and Kegan Paul. Copyright © David E. Scharff, 1982.

be rejecting at times; for instance, when she could not be there the instant that her infant wanted comfort or food. To cope with the intolerable feelings of anxiety and abandonment, the infant held on to her by taking the image of her as this rejecting object inside, a process called *introjection*. In Fairbairn's theory, introjection is the ego's first defense against unbearable pain and separation from the object. (In our view, however, infants internalize all aspects of the mothering relationship, because that is how they code experience from which they form psychological structure and become capable of separate functioning.)

WHERE DO SPLITTING AND REPRESSION FIT IN?

In Fairbairn's view, following introjection of the bad object, the infant now has a sense of dissatisfaction inside the rudimentary infant self. To retain undisturbed an ideal image of the mother in consciousness, the infant's ego deals with the pain of rejection by repressing the whole image of the unsatisfying object into unconsciousness. There the *rejected object* is further sorted into two categories, (1) the *rejecting object* and (2) the *exciting object*. However, an internal object cannot be split off and repressed by itself. The part of the ego that has to relate to that painful object has to be split off with the object, along with the affect that characterizes this painful relationship. In the case of the rejecting object, the relevant affects are anger, frustration, and sadness. In the case of the exciting object relationship, the affects are ones of craving and painful longing.

CAN YOU DESCRIBE THE REJECTING OBJECT RELATIONSHIP?

The rejecting object relationship consists of the antilibidinal ego, the rejecting object, and the affects of anger, rage, and sadness. Fairbairn originally called the part of the ego that was repressed with the rejecting object "the internal saboteur" because it threatened to return to consciousness and there spoil defensive idealization. Later Fairbairn changed the name of this part of the self to the *anti-libidinal ego*. The rejecting ego supports the central ego in further repressing the exciting object relationship. This sabotages the possibility of the central ego being invested with a good level of excitement about anticipating and seeking pleasant, vital relationships.

CAN YOU DESCRIBE THE EXCITING OBJECT RELATIONSHIP?

The other class of bad object relations — bad because painful, not morally bad — is the *need-exciting object relationship*. A good mother can excite need in her infant by being too attentive. She might anxiously hover near her infant or feed him too readily before he can feel his lust for food, comfort, and connection. Fairbairn's term for the object that excites need and desire is the *libidinal object* and for the part of the ego that relates to it, the *libidinal ego*. He chose these names to follow classical usage of the term *libido* to describe the sexual drives, which were thought by Freud to be the seat of all desire, but any correspondence is quite inexact. The affects that characterize the libidinal object relationship are ones of unsatisfiable longing, anxious arousal, and desperation.

CAN YOU GIVE AN EXAMPLE OF THE EXCITING AND REJECTING OBJECT RELATIONSHIPS?

Mrs. Constable, a tall, beautiful, and appealing woman, had been in therapy with me (JSS) for two years at the hospital outpatient clinic. By this time, we both knew that she carried the burden of an exciting object relationship derived from her infantile experience of prolonged and suddenly terminated breast-feeding with her mother. She perpetuated this object relationship with her own babies, at one point storming the hospital nursery to demand her sleeping newborn. She realized that she wanted the excitement of feeding her child because she felt lonely and scared in her hospital room. In later years her eldest boy developed a habit of letting his tongue hang out. Mrs. Constable felt revulsion at this habit and became quite phobic of his mouth in order to avoid the anger that she felt toward him. As treatment progressed, she understood that she was also avoiding her own feelings of emptiness, hunger, and neediness that his open mouth evoked in her. Here, a rejecting object relationship defended against the stimulation of the more painful and therefore more repressed exciting object relationship.

The constellation came to light in the transference in a vivid and violent way. Mrs. Constable missed her appointment time, which was the last one before I had to go to another job. Arriving at my office 20 minutes after the end of her session time, she coyly peeped around my half-open door and told me that she was sorry to have mistaken the time. Even though she could see that I was collecting my things to leave, she sweetly asked if I could see her. When I told her that I had to go to another appointment, Mrs. Constable pleaded with me seductively. When I said that we would have to miss this time and meet as usual in two days time, Mrs. Constable became enraged. She told me that I was cold and uncaring and began to hit me until she was restrained in the corridor by two male nurses who heard the commotion through the open office door. Seeing me apparently available had excited her need for me. When the exciting object relationship could not be gratified in relation to me, the rejecting object relationship was expressed in full force. When she arrived too late for me to see her, she had hoped to repress the inevitable activation of the rejecting object relationship by attempting to recruit me to the exciting object relationship where I would need to see her as much as she needed to see me and more than I needed to see my next patient. After this episode, she idealized the male nurses as strong men who really knew what she needed, while I was experienced as a horrible, weak, and unsatisfying woman. In her transference to me, the rejecting object relationship had to be worked on for months before she could experience me as helpful once more.

Thomas Ogden has suggested another term for the libidinal object relationship, namely the *craving self* that longs for a *tantalizing object*. Harry Guntrip pointed out that excessive activity of the libidinal part of the self may serve to cover over a dreadful sense of deadness at the center of the self, suggesting to him an even more deeply repressed part of the self.

IS THERE A MORE REPRESSED PART OF THE SELF THAN FAIRBAIRN KNEW ABOUT?

Fairbairn's original theory did not account for a part of the self more deeply repressed than the libidinal internal object system. Guntrip proposed that in schizoid states, a further subdivision of the already repressed libidinal ego is repressed and split off into a remote, deadened part of the self where it is harbored against the expected danger of empathic failure and the desperately frightening experience of a void within the core of the self. Fairbairn accepted Guntrip's important addendum to his theory. Michael Balint discovered a similar phenomenon in his regressed patients. They described a feeling of something missing at the core of the self. He called this the basic fault. These deficit states arise from a poor mother–infant relationship in which the infant did not feel cared for, loved, and lovable. Object relations theorists recognized that their discoveries had implications for technique. As Guntrip put it, therapy had to offer a challenge to the closed system of parts of the personality and present a context for rebirth and regrowth in the therapeutic relationship as an alternative to regression.

WHAT IS THE OBJECT RELATIONSHIP OF THE CENTRAL SELF IN CONSCIOUSNESS?

Late in his theory-building, Fairbairn described the object of the central self, discovered during his study of hysterical states. He called it the *ideal object*. In the hysterical state, it is an object shorn of excessive excitement or rejection. The hysterical person seeks in the lover a bland object so as not to be unbearably upset or excited. In the normal state, we think of the ideal object as an internal object that is satisfactory. We might call this the good-enough object, or simply, the good object. Nowadays, the terms *ideal, good,* and *good-enough* are used interchangeably. The ideal object is the object of the central ego and is connected to it by positive feelings in the full range of human affects, and it remains in consciousness because it is satisfying. The ideal object relationship in the central, conscious part of the self is available for interaction with ideal objects in other personalities. Being in consciousness, it is free to grow and be modified because it is not harbored secretly inside the self, as the repressed exciting and rejecting object relationships are. Nevertheless, the good object tends to be absorbed or metabolized by our central selves. The ideal object relationship suffuses the entire personality rather than standing out as a discrete, recognizable piece of psychic structure.

In the case of Mrs. Constable, the good object in relation to the central self gave rise to a central ideal object relationship that was expressed in her capacity to be an energetic mother and homemaker, a sought-after committee person, and a patient with the capacity to sustain a therapeutic alliance despite the assault of the return of the repressed bad object relationships in the transference.

Paradoxically, although it is in consciousness, the ideal object relationship is less observable than the repressed object, relationships that are expressed in the interpersonal field — and especially in the transference — in the form of unsatisfying relationships that call attention to them.

CAN YOU SUMMARIZE THE OBJECT RELATIONSHIPS IN ACTION?

The human personality is a system of conscious and unconscious object relationships in dynamic relation. The central ego actively represses the rejecting and exciting constellations. The antilibidinal ego further represses the exciting object constellation, and the libidinal ego further represses the rejecting object constellation. A further split may occur in which an endangered part of the libidinal ego is further repressed and becomes deeply withdrawn. Now we can summarize the endopsychic situation as follows: (1) *in consciousness,* the *ideal object relationship,* consisting of the central ego, the ideal object, and feelings of satisfaction and goodness; (2) *in unconsciousness,* the *rejecting object relationship,* consisting of the antilibidinal ego, the rejecting object, and feelings of frustration and rage; and the *exciting object relationship,* consisting of the libidinal ego, the exciting object, and feelings of frustration and painful longing.

COULD YOU ELABORATE ON THE SELF?

The self is the original psychic structure the person is born with. It then matures and develops by building into it traces of important and formative relationships. As it does this, the self becomes the encompassing structure that includes not only its original potential for structure but also a sense of identity based on all the internal object relations within it. The ideal, exciting and rejecting objects, the central, libidinal, and antilibidinal parts of the ego in relationship to these objects, respectively, as well as the whole collection of corresponding affects are all in an internal dynamic relationship to each other. This dynamic relation between parts of the self follows the universal system of the endopsychic situation that Fairbairn described, but the precise balance of forces is unique to each person.

HOW IS IT THAT INTERNAL OBJECT RELATIONSHIPS ARE IN DYNAMIC RELATION?

Fairbairn described how one part of internal structure represses another part directly and indirectly. The central ego represses both the exciting and rejecting object constellations directly. Then the rejecting object constellation (that is, the internal saboteur and the rejecting object together) lies on top of the libidinal object like a blanket keeping it out of awareness of the central ego. Fairbairn said that repression happens in this direction rather than the reverse, because it is much more painful to be aware of an unrequited longing than to have an angry relationship. On the contrary, we find that it is equally common for the libidinal or excited object relationship to repress rejecting object relations. We see this in a person who has a seductive attitude toward others as a defensive way of repressing aggression or feelings of rejection. We see it in married partners who seduce each other to be sexually intimate in order to avoid angry feelings that cannot be expressed.

When Fairbairn described the secondary repression of the libidinal by the antilibidinal constellations inside the self, he opened the door for us to understand that internal object relationships inside the self are in dynamic relationship to each other, so that at one point one constellation will be the controlling or ascendant organization, and at another point a different one will come to the fore. This is a crucial discovery that informs the clinical approach to patients. We find that we are dealing with parts of the patient's self and that we are being used to re-create now one object relationship and now another.

Is the Self the Same as the Ego?

Not in our view. Some people have said that the self is the more modern term for the old-fashioned term *ego*. Guntrip used the term *self* that way, and John Sutherland in his teaching was inclined to follow Guntrip's usage. In our lexicon, *self* is an overall term for that continuing sense of uniqueness that a person carries. We think that the term *self* includes ego, that is to say, the executive relating function and both its conscious and unconscious aspects, the objects that the parts of the ego relate to, and all the feelings that arise between the parts of the ego and parts of the object.

Do You Use the Word *Ego*, then, for the More Mechanistic Part of Each of Us that Performs Certain Executive Functions but Is Not Capable of Relating as a Whole Person?

Yes, the ego is an executive subset of the self. Only the self can relate as a whole person.

NOTES

Fairbairn (1963) condensed his verbal description of intrapsychic organization on one page. His key concepts of internal object relations appear as follows:

The internal saboteur (1944).

The libidinal and antilibidinal ego (1954, 1963).

The ideal object (1954, 1963).

Others have elaborated related ideas:

The craving self and the tantalizing object (Ogden 1986b).

The withdrawn libidinal ego in schizoid states (Guntrip 1969).

The self (Guntrip 1969, Sutherland 1980).

FOUR

Projective and Introjective Identification and Containment

AFTER INTROJECTION OF THE OBJECT, SPLITTING, AND REPRESSION, WHAT ARE THE OTHER IMPORTANT MECHANISMS OF UNCONSCIOUS ORGANIZATION AND COMMUNICATION BETWEEN PERSONALITIES?

The mechanisms of projective and introjective identification were described by Melanie Klein in 1946, later clarified by Hanna Segal, and elaborated by Thomas Ogden, Joseph Sandler, and, more recently, by Jill Scharff. Projective and introjective identification are psychic mechanisms that serve communicative, defensive, and organizational functions. They begin in the earliest months of life, when the infant is struggling with great anxiety stemming from fears for its life and worries that the force of its feelings will overwhelm the caretaker on whom it is totally dependent. In projective identification the infant exports these anxieties in the form of fantasies of putting dangerous parts of itself into the mother for control of aggression. The mother is then identified with these projected, or displaced, parts of the self. This is the first phase of the projective identification process. The infant then fears that feelings that might have overwhelmed it had they remained within the infant self will now return to haunt it in the form of a mother who has been suffused with these frightening feelings. The mother is then seen as a retaliatory object. This is the second phase of the projective identification process. Now the infant takes in this view of the mother through introjective identification, which is the third phase of the projective identification process. The infant now becomes more like the frightening mother and has even more fearsome feelings to get rid of. The good-enough mother, however, is able to metabolize these worrisome feelings, to cope with them and to return to the infant a view of himself as not overly damaging or endangered. Wilfred Bion described the mother's process as *containment* of her child's anxieties.

The infant also projects into the mother valued aspects of the self for safekeeping of the good. The mother is also suffused by the infant's good feelings toward her and gives back to her child a loving, gratifying sense of himself. Putting out and taking back appreciated goodness and detoxified badness is the infant's way of building a relationship and forming a durable personality.

Projective and introjective identification are reciprocal processes inside the self and also between the self and the external object. Projective identification originates from both the mother and the baby. The mutuality of the projective and introjective identificatory processes between mother and child are shown in Figure 4-1.

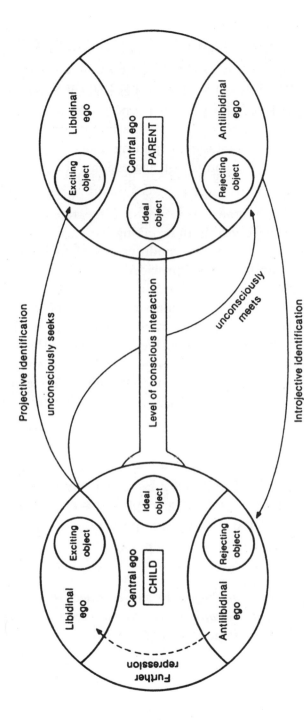

FIG. 4-1. Projective and introjective identification. The mechanism here is the interaction of the child's projective and introjective identifications with the parent as the child meets frustration, unrequited yearning, or trauma. The diagram depicts the child longing to have his needs met and identifying with similar trends in the parent via projective identification. If he meets with rejection, he identifies with the frustration of the parent's own antilibidinal system via introjective identification. In an internal reaction to the frustration, the libidinal system is further repressed by the renewed force of the child's antilibidinal system.

Reprinted from *The Sexual Relationship: An Object Relations View of Sex and the Family,* courtesy of Routledge and Kegan Paul.

Copyright © David E. Scharff, 1982.

Can You Say More About the Introjective Identification Subphase of Projective Identification?

Introjective identification is also to be regarded as a process in its own right. We have found that it tends to be overlooked because it happens inside the ego. It is easier to see how the object is being affected than to detect internalizations that are integrated into the self; putting out is more visible than taking in. In introjective identification, infants take in that modification of their earlier feelings that their mothers have provided. They take in the experiences and build them into a more mature view of themselves. If the mothers are not able to contain their infants' worries, the babies then receive a view of themselves that confirms their poor sense of themselves as unmanageable. When the mothers are good enough, they take in their mothers' good containing function and then become able to manage themselves and their feelings, now and in the future, in a progressively more competent and reliable way.

Can You Summarize the Steps of the Process of Projective and Introjective Identification?

These steps are amplified in *Projective and Introjective Identification and the Use of the Therapist's Self*. We can reduce them to their main components, summarized in Table 4–1.

Table 4–1. The Steps of Projective Identification
1. Projecting or getting rid of a part of the self
2. Finding it in the object, that is, experiencing the other person as embodying that part of oneself, whether the person happens to be like that or not
3. Taking in and becoming like the object that was projected into

CAN YOU SAY MORE ABOUT CONTAINMENT?

Containment is a term introduced by Wilfred Bion. It refers to the mother's ability to hold her baby and his needs in her mind. Bion thought that this ability belonged to the realm of thought, but we think of containment as an integrated emotional and cognitive process. The baby has various unmanageable anxieties that, in the Kleinian way of looking at things, stem from the "death instinct," or, in our own way of thinking, from aggression and its excesses. The baby, not able to manage these anxieties, puts them into the mother, who "contains" them in her maternal state of "reverie" and is not destroyed by the force of the aggression. Through a transformation of the disorganized elements of baby experience into thought made possible by this state of reverie, the mother can then feed back to the infant the unthinkable anxiety in a more manageable, tolerable form. Bion used the term *contained* for these originally overwhelming anxieties that the mother then helps the infant to manage. He referred to the mother as the container.

Taking off from Bion's idea, we think that containment occurs through resonance with the mother's own internal object relations. Through normal projective identification, she matches her child's anxieties with her own partly repressed internal object relationships, and then, by being able to bear or even appreciate her own and her child's anxiously viewed parts herself, she gives them back safely to her infant, along with her capacity for tolerance.

NOTES

Klein's concept of the unconscious processes of introjective and projective identification have revolutionized our conceptualization of therapeutic action. These processes deserve study both in the original and in the following expositions:

Projective and introjective identification (Klein 1946, Segal 1964, Ogden 1982, Sandler 1987a,b, J. Scharff 1992).

Containment and reverie (Bion 1962, 1967).

FIVE

The Holding Environment

The mothering function is addressed from a different vantage point by Donald Winnicott. He referred to the quality of the actual relationship offered by the mother to her infant in which the infant could expect a secure and stable relationship with a mother committed to providing for his needs. Winnicott was not referring to an internal processing function but to a physical care-taking relationship characterized by "primary maternal pre-occupation" with and devotion to her infant. He used the term *holding environment* to describe this process, within which the mother provided a *holding relationship*. Winnicott thought that the mother's capacity to provide this secure holding relationship in her role as the *environment mother* was what let the infant find its self. Then, the infant self could relate to the mother as an object of love and aggression, *the object mother*.

HOW IS THE TERM *CONTAINMENT* DIFFERENT FROM *HOLDING ENVIRONMENT?*

Winnicott is concerned with the management of the space between the mother and the baby, whereas Bion is referring to the space inside the mother in which she processes her baby's anxieties. Winnicott's terms *holding* and *handling* are visible elements of an external process that is observable, whereas Bion's term *containment* describes an internal process in the realm of thought. Winnicott is dealing with the interpersonal aspect, Bion with the intrapsychic dimension of the two individuals.

Now we have two contributions that need to be put together to constitute the whole process. We stress that the mother holds the baby in the physical and emotional sense. According to Winnicott, as the object mother she provides an intimate relationship for her baby, and as the environment mother she takes care of the environment so that the baby can feel safe and is able to "go on being." At the same time, a psychological process is going on inside herself in which she absorbs, or in Bion's word, *contains,* those anxieties that the baby inevitably faces. It is the process outside, namely the holding environment, that sets the stage for the internal process, namely containment, to occur inside the mother and later to be taken in by the baby. Both internal and external processes have to occur at the same time for the baby to handle anxiety well and so have a maximal chance of undisturbed development.

What Are Some Of The Other Concepts That Winnicott Contributed To Using British Object Relations Theory As A Clinical Approach?

Winnicott gives us several other concepts that are both theoretically and clinically useful: the centrality of the mother–infant relationship, the object mother, the environment mother, the psychosomatic partnership, the transitional space and transitional objects, and the fit between true and false self.

The centrality of the mother–infant relationship

Winnicott focused on the centrality of the mother–infant relationship, the context in which the baby becomes a person. He said that there was no such thing as a mother without a baby. He emphasized the importance of the mother–infant relationship for personal development and he described its re-creation in the transference. We do not mean to suggest that a person is fully formed during the preoedipal relationship to the mother. People continue to be modified by new relationships throughout life, but primary relationships always exert a continuing influence on personality structure.

The object mother and the environment mother

Winnicott described two important aspects of relating in the mother–infant relationship. In the first aspect the mother formed the context for the baby's growth and development. This he called the *environment mother*. Providing an "arms-around" relationship, the environment mother holds the baby in her arms, sets the conditions for keeping the baby fed, clothed, warm, and safe, and takes care of the physical and emotional environment for the baby. If all goes well, the baby takes the environment mother for granted and just "goes on being."

Within the envelope provided by the environment mother, the mother offers the baby a direct object relationship. Winnicott called this aspect the *object mother*. This mother is the object of the baby's love, hate, interest, and desire. It is apparent that both parts of the mother are always present, and that we can distinguish them for purposes of understanding which function the mother is fulfilling at a certain time. Within the envelope provided by the environment mother, the baby is free to find its self. In the relationship with the mother as an object, the baby is provided with the stuff from which to build its own internal objects. From experience of the relationship between the environment mother and the object mother and between the whole mother and the infant, the infant develops its internalized object relationships and sense of self.

The psychosomatic partnership

Winnicott also contributed the idea of the *psychosomatic partnership*. The earliest relationship to the mother is completely physical, when the fetus lives literally inside the mother. At the moment of birth, a physical and emotional interface develops across which mother and baby then have to relate. The baby becomes psychologically organized through its sorting of the experience of physical holding and handling.

Transitional space and transitional objects

Over the first few months, this physical relationship gives way to a progressively larger psychological relationship. It does so with the creation of what Winnicott called the *potential space* between mother and baby. We tend to refer to this as the *transitional space*. In this space, the baby relates to the mother across a growing physical distance. Here, the baby is free to discover the things the mother is offering as though the baby had been the one to invent or create them. Winnicott says that we must never challenge the baby to resolve the paradox of whether something was offered by the mother or invented by the infant. We maintain respect for the infant's illusion of separateness as the basis for true autonomy and for the creative potential of the transitional space. In this space, the baby has *transitional objects,* such as a favorite blanket or teddy bear, which belong to the baby entirely and are used and abused, held and thrown, loved and hated as the baby's own, and yet they represent the mother. By interacting with the transitional object, the baby can act as if it is in full control of its object mother.

In figure 5-1, we can see that the transitional space is a blend of inner and outer experience. It is in communication with the

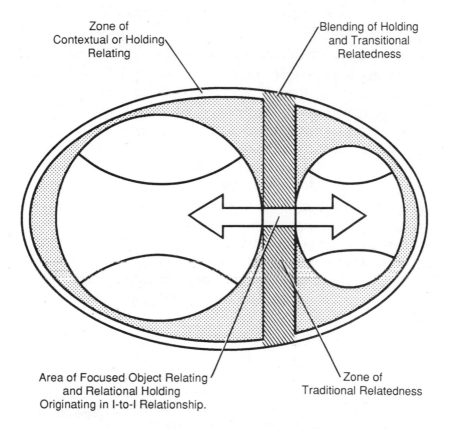

Zone of Contextual or Holding Relating

Blending of Holding and Transitional Relatedness

Area of Focused Object Relating and Relational Holding Originating in I-to-I Relationship.

Zone of Traditional Relatedness

FIG. 5-1. Winnicott's organization of the mother–infant relationship. Reproduced from *Refinding the Object and Reclaiming the Self,* courtesy of Jason Aronson Inc. Copyright © David E. Scharff, 1992.

The psychosomatic partnership begins with a physical holding-and-handling relationship between mother and infant. The oval envelope drawn around mother and infant signifies the environmental function provided by the mother's holding—the *arms-around* relationship. Within this envelope, mother and infant have a direct object relationship—the intense I-to-I relationship, communicated in words, gestures, gaze, and physical exchange—out of which the infant constructs its internal objects.

holding provided by the mother, just as it is in communication with the direct object relationship to the mother, that provides the material of the baby's growing internal world. Winnicott noted that this space is also the locus of creativity.

WHAT IS WINNICOTT'S CONCEPT OF *TRUE AND FALSE SELF?*

Winnicott thought that each of us has an inner core that stems from our biological givens. He called this the *true self*. The false self is a caretaker part of the self that protects the core and enables the self to accommodate to the needs of others. It is not false in the sense of being fake or untrustworthy. It is simply cover for the true self. When childrearing emphasizes the needs of others at the expense of the self, there is then a discrepancy between the false self and the true self. A denial of the true self results, and the cover appears to be untrue to the true self. In pathology, the false self becomes false in the sense of being somewhat fake. In health, the false self is not so split off from the true self. It successfully enables us to preserve our selfhood while negotiating with others. As Christopher Bollas notes, good fit between false self and true self is essential to the maintenance of personal vitality and integrity.

NOTES

Winnicott's concepts, derived from his experience as a pediatrician and analyst of the mother–infant relationship, are to be found in the following papers or books:
    Primary maternal preoccupation (1956).
    Holding environment, holding relationship, holding and handling, and the centrality of the mother–infant relationship (1960).
    Environment mother and object mother (1945, 1963a, 1963b).
    Psychosomatic partnership (1971).
    Potential space and transitional objects (1951).
    True and false self (1965, and Bollas 1989b).

For a thorough overview of Winnicott's concepts, see Phillips (1988) and Grolnick (1990).

SIX

The Concept of Positions and Attachment Theory

Melanie Klein described two fundamental positions, the paranoid-schizoid position and the depressive position. These offer an alternative or parallel view to Sigmund Freud's psychosexual stages of development. Klein arrived at her ideas from study of the infant–mother relationship, re-created in the transference. Her ideas are taught both in clinical supervision and in discussion of direct observation of mother–baby couples.

The *paranoid-schizoid position* occurs during the first few months of life, when the infant faces a maximal amount of anxiety with a minimal cognitive processing apparatus. Gradually learning from experience and maturing cognitively, the infant becomes capable of more advanced functioning typical of the depressive position.

In the paranoid-schizoid position, the infant's relationships are dominated by splitting and repression with projection of aggression. The resulting object relationships are therefore part object relationships, characterized by all-or-none qualities. The mother is seen by the infant as good or bad, or more precisely as a good or bad breast, in keeping with the part object ascendancy at this stage. She is spoiled in fantasy by angry oral, urethral or anal outpourings. Part of her is loved, and another part hated, but she cannot be loved and hated at the same time, because the infant is not capable of seeing her as a whole person. It is in this position that splitting and pathological degrees of projective identification predominate, as the infant's ways of defending against anxiety and as modes of relating.

The *depressive position* is a major development that begins by about 3 or 4 months of age. The maturing baby periodically moves beyond splitting, projection, and the resulting all-or-none quality of early relationships, toward a state of concern for its object. The child becomes cognitively capable of a more complete image of the mother as a whole person who is capable of embodying good and bad, loving and rejecting qualities. The new capacity for holding in mind the good, present mother and the absent or bad mother at the same time means that splitting is no longer the only option for dealing with pain. Pain can now be borne by reliance on the internalized good object. Once it is reliably inside the self, the infant becomes able to tolerate ambivalence, to experience guilt about being responsible for the way that the object has been treated, and to repair the harm done. Early aspects of envy prominent in the paranoid-schizoid position are modified by guilt about, concern for, and gratitude toward the object, and the wish to make up to or "repair" relationship with the object. Working through of depressive and persecutory anxieties continues through the first few years of childhood.

IS THE PARANOID-SCHIZOID POSITION ONE THAT A PERSON GROWS OUT OF AND THEN MOVES INTO THE DEPRESSIVE POSITION AS A SIGN OF HEALTH?

Once these positions come on line, they are present through the rest of the life cycle. We do not totally grow out of the paranoid-schizoid position into the depressive position, but the more mature person functions more often in the depressive end of the range. Both positions are potentially operative, normally and pathologically. As adults, we continue to move between them. Both of them are positions from which to deal with the world, and each has its assets and liabilities. The paranoid-schizoid position is the basis of psychosis but also promotes an inquiring and sometimes suitably untrusting approach to the outer world. The depressive position enables us to have concern for others, to empathize, to make up for having harmed others who are important to us, and to accept loss and reality. The depressive position need not imply the presence of a depressed mood. It refers to a capacity to tolerate depression due to guilt and loss, and to experience concern for the object.

Klein also described the "manic defense." A person who cannot bear guilt and yet who has progressed beyond paranoid-schizoid functioning may jump over the depressive position in order to avoid the painful realization of damage done to the object that comes with the depressive position. Instead of feeling concern for the harmed object, the person controls the object contemptuously and denies its separateness, its suffering, and the ambivalence that it evokes. Concern for the object may be mimicked in a manic repair attempt that covers over the effect on the object and serves to avoid responsibility for one's effect on others.

ARE THESE THE ONLY POSSIBLE POSITIONS?

These are the two that Klein described. More recently, Thomas Ogden studied the work of Esther Bick, Donald Meltzer, Frances Tustin and several other contributors and integrated their work with his own to come up with an even earlier position that he calls the *autistic-contiguous position.*

The autistic-contiguous position refers to the baby's need to be next to an object in order to define the self-boundary. The baby uses its proximity to the physically well-defined edges of its caretaker in order to define both the physical body self and the internal psychological contours. Like the other two positions, the autistic-contiguous position remains throughout life.

Through life, we move among these three positions along the continuum from primacy of self to concern for objects. We are preoccupied at our most anxious times with development and cohesion of the self (*autistic-contiguous position*), at more mature times with the case of our whole, ambivalently loved object (*depressive position*). Between times, we struggle against feared retaliation from split-off, repressed bad part-objects (*paranoid-schizoid position*) (see Figure 6–1).

HOW DOES BRITISH OBJECT RELATIONS THEORY RELATE TO ATTACHMENT THEORY DEVELOPED FROM INFANT RESEARCH BY BOWLBY?

John Bowlby, a researcher with a background in analysis and ethology, studied our biological "givens" and the centrality of the need to be in a nurturing relationship for the healthy development of the human and other mammals. He contributed *attachment theory,* the basis for much of the modern research into infant development and the mother–infant relationship. He took an ethological (or animal behavior) approach and made a convincing argument that the infant in the human species and in all the higher mammalian species needs a relationship to the mother for survival. Then he viewed behavior in terms of anxiety about nearness to and separation from the mother. He found that issues of attachment and loss are central and that the nature of their resolution determines personality development and psychopathology. His work establishes the primacy of problems of separation from and loss of a parent in the development of most psychopathological conditions.

AUTISTIC/CONTIGUOUS POSITION ⇄ PARANOID/SCHIZOID POSITION ⇄ DEPRESSIVE POSITION

FIG. 6-1. The Continuum of Endopsychic Positions.

NOTES

Klein studied unconscious fantasy and communication between infant and mother. She found that because of destructive anxiety, the infant relates to the mother as a part-object and only later becomes capable of keeping the mother as a whole object in mind and feeling concern for her. These two states of mind persist throughout life as potential ways of relating. They are discussed in the following works:

The paranoid schizoid position and the depressive position, splitting and projection (Klein 1946).

The manic defense, concern and repair (Klein 1935).

Ogden integrated the earlier work of Bick (1968, 1986), Tustin (1981, 1984, 1986) and Meltzer (1975) to arrive at his concept of the autistic-contiguous position (Ogden 1989).

These intrapsychic positions are achieved in the context of the infant's attachment to the mother.

Attachment theory (Bowlby 1969, 1973, 1980).

SEVEN

Object Relations Theory as a Way of Working

HOW DOES OBJECT RELATIONS THEORY HELP US IN CLINICAL PRACTICE?

Our mentor, the late Jock Sutherland, liked to say that object relations is not so much a theory as a way of working. Object relations theory puts the relationship between the therapist and the patient at the center of the way of working. While the therapist and patient join together in the task of examining the patient's internal world and its effect on the patient's relationships, at the same time the patient and therapist are in a relationship themselves. This therapeutic relationship forms the laboratory in which the therapist learns most centrally about the patient's ways of relating and the difficulties they include. As the therapist processes the experience of this current relationship, he or she is able to inform the patient about this experience. In this way, patient and therapist have a current shared relationship that both can study and learn from.

The patient (or the group of patients when we see a family, couple, or therapy group) establishes a current relationship with the therapist that reflects the internal object relations set that is brought to all relationships. In therapy, we take it as our task to experience these current expressions of object relationships in the interpersonal field. As therapists we experience them within ourselves in terms of fantasies or feelings that are somewhat foreign to us and that arise within us specifically in response to the patient before us. This way of working is characterized by the use of what Sigmund Freud termed *transference* and *countertransference.*

WHAT IS TRANSFERENCE?

In object relations terms, *transference* is the patient's projective identification in the clinical setting. Freud described the way that a patient would aim the drives at the therapist as a new edition of the original target. At first, Freud thought that the transference got in the way of therapy because it muddied the waters, but he quickly came to see that the phenomenon of transference was what gave the therapist a living example of the way the patient coped with forbidden thoughts and feelings. In object relations theory, we do not see transference as the displacement of primitive impulses, as Freud suggested. We see transference as the expression of internal object relationships experienced externally in the therapeutic relationship.

HOW ABOUT COUNTERTRANSFERENCE?

Freud originally used the term *countertransference* to refer to those feelings and attitudes stirred up in the therapist as a result of the therapist's unresolved difficulties. These, therefore, interfered with the therapist's capacity to remain neutral and helpful. Freud did not develop his idea of countertransference as fully as he did that of transference. We've already noticed how he began by thinking of transference as an impediment and later came to see it as the principal vehicle of analysis. Countertransference can be seen the same way. Freud originally described countertransference as an impediment to work, but modern object relations therapists have come to see it as the vehicle for therapeutic interaction and the basis of understanding and interpretation. The set of feelings and attitudes stirred up in the therapist form a model of what happens inside the people with whom the patient is in relationship. Providing that therapists have been well trained and have had personal therapy so that their own personal issues do not interfere prominently, they are then in the position to use their internal experience with their patients to make sense of the patients' ways of relating. Therefore, we expect object relations therapists to monitor their internal states of feeling and the ideas, associations, and fantasies that occur to them during treatment in order to make sense of the relationship with the patient. While we do not advise a therapist to report these experiences in raw and unmetabolized form to a patient, we do expect that the therapist will examine them thoughtfully as the best set of clues as to the patient's problems in relating in depth, and will then use the countertransference to inform the ensuing interpretation of the transference.

WHAT CONSTITUTES THE TECHNIQUE OF OBJECT RELATIONS THEORY?

There is not a series of separate techniques to be applied systematically, like communications or behavioral techniques. The technique of object relations therapy comprises a set of attitudes that set the frame and hold it steady to allow the emergence of an in-depth, committed therapeutic relationship. This relationship offers a transference–countertransference microcosm in which to display, experience, and modify the patient's internal object relations difficulties over the span of the treatment. There is not a right or wrong way of working so much as a set of conditions to be met in order to enable a relationship to grow and deepen.

NOTES

The technique of object relations theory is not a series of maneuvers. Instead, it comprises a set of attitudes derived from individual and group analytic concepts. The practice of object relations therapy relies on transference and countertransference:

Object relations way of working (Sutherland 1980).

Transference (Freud 1905, 1915b, 1917b).

Countertransference (Freud 1910a).

Transference and countertransference (D. Scharff and J. Scharff 1987).

EIGHT

Relation to Other Theoretical Systems and Clinical Approaches

HOW DOES BRITISH OBJECT RELATIONS THEORY RELATE TO OTHER THEORIES?

British object relations theory is one of the psychoanalytic theories of the personality.

HOW IS IT THE SAME AS AND DIFFERENT FROM FREUD'S CLASSICAL PSYCHOANALYTIC THEORY?

It is the same in that it rests on the same secure base that Sigmund Freud's theory provided, but it is different in that it has departed from the instinctual basis of that theory. Freud held that the human is motivated by inner instinctual sexual and aggressive drives that aim for discharge and gratification by the available object (namely, the mother) so that the personality can return to a comfortable state of being in which homeostasis is restored. He thought that the human seeks objects principally to gratify impulses. In contrast, British object relations theory holds that the human infant is motivated by the need to be in relationship with the mother and the father, separately and as a couple, and with important family members. Object relations theorists see the drives as deriving their meaning and energy in the context of relationships. They notice the phenomena of sexual and aggressive impulse discharges outside the context of relationships, but instead of regarding these as instinctual, they see them as the products of relationship breakdown rather than the building blocks of relationships.

Despite this fundamental difference in theory, Freudian theory and British object relations theory in practice share a number of techniques, including working with the unconscious, following the affect, valuing insight, dealing with transference, working with dreams and fantasy material, and communicating most effectively through interpretation. British object relations theory, however, puts more emphasis on analysis of the counter-transference as the vehicle for understanding the patient's personality difficulties.

IS OBJECT RELATIONS THEORY LIKE KOHUT'S SELF PSYCHOLOGY THEORY?

Both of these theories are interested in the development of the self and how it is affected by the quality of the object. Both recognize that our capacity to understand the object is much advanced over our capacity to understand the self. Since the self is a private thing experienced only inside oneself, it is much harder to observe that self in action than it is to observe the action of the internal object relationships that are being expressed in the interpersonal realm. Both theories value introspection and empathy, but self psychology emphasizes the concept of empathic understanding based on the therapist's attunement to and identification with the patient's self, while object relations theory uses countertransference both to parts of the patient's self and to the various objects contained within it. Object relations theory uses the concept of projective identification to conceptualize the therapeutic re-creation of the internal object relationships in the transference.

In object relations theory, internal objects are in relation to parts of the self, bound together by affects, resulting in internal object relationships that are in dynamic relation. In self psychology, a theory put forth by Heinz Kohut, the self contains self-objects. The self-object is a psychic structure in which the internal object is used to support the cohesion of the self and to regulate the self's sense of well-being and self-esteem. Kohut's theory has usefully extended our understanding of the use of internal and external objects in clinical conditions due to problems of the self, namely, splitting of the self in borderline states and narcissistic personality disorders. It has informed the therapist's sensitivity as to how to become the necessary object for such a patient. Similarly, Harry Guntrip, an object relations theorist, has contributed to understanding the splitting of the self that results when the libidinal ego has deeply regressed to the point of withdrawal, resulting in a sense of loss of the self. Like Kohut, he recommended the provision of a therapeutic relationship sensitively attuned to this level of self-functioning. Both theories agree that the security of the self lies at the center of psychological health, but object relations theory regards the self-object, that is, the one-way use of an object as a support for the self, not as a healthy structure but as a breakdown in the mutuality of self and object in a relationship in which each should be of use to the other. Self psychology has not explored the reciprocity between self and object, and therefore we have found it less applicable than object relations theory to couple and family therapy, although Marion Solomon and Mel Lansky have used it in treatment of the borderline and narcissistic marriage.

Kohut's exploration of the development of the self and the way that a person needs his or her objects as self-objects in order to form a coherent, reliable, and matured self is a great contribution to the understanding of the development of the self and to the therapist's role in clinical work focused on problems of the self. These supplement Guntrip's work on deep schizoid problems focusing on loss of the self.

In summary, the work of Kohut and his school focused exclusively on the use by one person's self of the self-object. In object relations theory, we are interested in reciprocity, that is, wherever there is a self relating to an object, there is also an object relating to the self. When one person relates to another, the process is mutual, and resulting interactional and interpersonal process affects the development of both persons involved. Reciprocity between self and object occurs simultaneously in the interpersonal and intrapsychic realms. When the self psychologists consider all problems to relate to the coherence and resilience of the self using the self object, they consider only one-half of this mutual and resonating process. So self psychology has been particularly useful in understanding the problem of narcissism, whereas object relations theory has been criticized for assuming relatedness.

DOESN'T TOO MUCH EMPHASIS ON PROJECTIVE IDENTIFICATION OVERLOOK PROBLEMS OF NARCISSISM?

Yes. We can be so engaged in problems of how the self deals with its objects that we can overlook problems of how the self relates to itself as its primary object. In narcissism there is an insistence that the other person be there to service and admire oneself and a simultaneous conviction or despair that the other will not be willing or able to do so. So the person has to find this within the self. Then the self's inner world predominates over the interests of the other person. The intrapsychic dimension is not in free communication with the interpersonal field.

We see narcissism as a state of blocked projective identification. The narcissistic person is unable to use the healthy end of the projective identification continuum to develop empathy for others and has little capacity for introspection based on having understood the self in relation to others and their experience. In narcissistic self-relating, the self cannot take in a suitable object and introjectively identify with it.

Too much emphasis on projective identification also overlooks the process of introjective identification, an equally important psychic mechanism that has been largely ignored. Introjective identification refers to the taking in of experience with others and using it to build psychic structure. The process of introjective identification operates along a continuum from healthy selective identification to pathological, excessive, unintegrated introjection. Since introjective identification is happening inside the self, it is harder for us to see it occurring than projective identification, which can be noted in terms of its effects on objects outside the self. In narcissism, the self is stuck without the normal cycle of mutually influential projective and introjective identificatory processes shaping the personality, interacting with the outer world, adapting, accommodating to others, and developing a modified reality within the self.

HOW IS BRITISH OBJECT RELATIONS DIFFERENT FROM THE AMERICAN OBJECT RELATIONS THEORY OF KERNBERG, MAHLER, JACOBSON, AND MASTERSON?

In addition to a formidable grasp of Freudian psychoanalytic theory, including American ego psychology, Otto Kernberg knew the work of Klein, Fairbairn, and Bion especially thoroughly. He used Edith Jacobson's work as the springboard from which he blended American ego psychology with British object relations theory. Donald Rinsley based his object relations approach on Fairbairn. The developmental research of Margaret Mahler on the phases of separation and individuation of the infant from the mother contributed to understanding the development of object relations in early childhood. Taken together, these theoretical contributions have been the mainstream of American object relations notably applied by James Masterson to the treatment of character disorders, especially borderline personality syndromes.

British object relations theorists have not been interested in accommodating their theory to theories of drive and the development of the ego. They believe that most problems in human development and psychology concern the relationship between the self and its internal and external objects. Problems of ego functioning and adaptation that captured American interest are simply not focused upon. The intense interest in the use of transference and countertransference that characterizes British object relations therapy has not been echoed in the American clinical approach until recently.

British object relations theory views projective identification as a process with both normal and pathological aspects occurring along a continuum from health to paranoia, whereas in Kernberg's object relations theory, projective identification is almost always a psychotic or borderline phenomenon. Getting down to the technical nitty gritty, in Kernberg's theory splitting is viewed as a more primitive mechanism of defense than is repression, which is regarded as typical of higher-level neurotic conditions. In British object relations theory, splitting and repression are regarded as mechanisms that occur simultaneously in the formation of psychic structure; there cannot be one without the other.

In British object relations theory, there is less emphasis on diagnostic category. Splitting and repression are processes common to us all and are not divided up along diagnostic lines.

HOW DOES GROUP THEORY INFLUENCE OBJECT RELATIONS THERAPY?

Group theory is quite crucial to the object relations approach. It amplifies the interpersonal expression of intrapsychic object relationships and it has given us the ability to apply object relations theory to the conjoint therapies (family, couple, and group therapy). The original group studies from which we draw are those of S. H. Foulkes and Wilfred Bion.

Bion held that a group has a conscious level of task organization in which the group cooperates with the leader's instructions to get the job done. The group also has an unconscious level of functioning, organized not by the task or the leader, but by subgroups that form according to assumptions about how to get shared needs met by the group, if not by the leader. Bion noted that various individuals in a group were attracted to each other to form these subgroups. He used the term *valency* for the individual's propensity for instantaneous combination with others in subgroupings. Bion described three main categories of subgroup formations organized around basic assumptions that sometimes supported the task but more commonly interfered with it.

Table 8–1. Bion's Basic Assumptions of Group Life
1. Dependency
2. Fight/flight
3. Pairing to create a savior

In basic-assumption dependency, the group is dominated by a subgroup that expresses needs to be cared for and directed by the leader. In basic-assumption fight/flight, the subgroup is angry at the leader for not making everything perfect and wants to fight his authority, flee from the task that he set, or select a new leader or task. In basic-assumption pairing, the group that is frustrated because individuals cannot have preferred pairing relationships with the leader produces two individuals who pair instead. The fantasy is that theirs will be a creative pairing to produce a new leader who will save the group.

Our experience with family groups confirms the validity of Bion's basic assumptions and leads us to add a more basic assumption to Bion's list:

Table 8–2. Bion's Basic Assumptions Expanded
1. Dependency
2. Fight/flight
3. Pairing to create a savior
4. Fission/fusion

We find this assumption of fission/fusion operating in the threatened family that regresses to a state of primitive merging (fusion) or splintering of the membership (fission). In fusion, merging substitutes for understanding and conflict resolution, whereas in fission, conflict attacks linking and murders understanding. Like a group of people in group therapy, the family that is stuck in dealing with its developmental task can learn in family therapy to detect the basic-assumption interference and attend to their unconscious needs and fears, so that the family can return to its current developmental work.

Bion himself made no explicit integration of his group work with his individual theory-building about in-depth unconscious communication. Putting together his individual concept of containment with his group theory of valency and basic-assumption functioning, we can see that individuals are in unconscious communication with others based on their shared object relations. The individual develops psychic structure from experiences in important primary groups—the family, the peer group, and the work group. The individual continues to find groups in which to live and work and grow throughout the life cycle.

Foulkes pointed out that each member of a group acts like a node in a grid. He said that the individual incorporates the group, and at the same time the group reflects aspects of the individual. Integrating and applying Foulkes's and Bion's ideas to group behavior, we can describe the expression of individuals' internal object relations. The group, like the individual, has a system of conscious and unconscious parts in dynamic relation. The individual is a system that includes an internal group.

HOW CAN OBJECT RELATIONS THERAPY BE INTEGRATED WITH A SYSTEMS APPROACH TO COUPLES AND FAMILIES?

Again, group theory is the key. The individual grows not only in relation to a mother, as so many theories emphasize, but grows within a family group. The individual takes in the experience with this family group to build an internal group of object relationships in a dynamic system. Thus the individual personality can be seen as comprising an internal system that then creates interaction with other internal systems in significant others. In this way object relations theory provides a bridge between individual, couple, and family treatment.

HOW CAN THE ECLECTIC FAMILY THERAPIST ALREADY USING AN ACTIVE SYSTEMIC METHOD INTEGRATE THE NONDIRECTIVE OBJECT RELATIONS APPROACH WITH AN APPROACH THAT IS QUITE DIRECTIVE AND CONTROLLING OF THE THERAPEUTIC INTERACTION?

The object relations approach advises therapists to try not to do too much. This can be a major challenge for those who are committed to an extremely interventionist model. If family therapists are interested in learning more from families as to how to proceed, perhaps they will find it useful to back off and wait for the direction to emerge from within the here-and-now experience.

Leading family therapists describe a change in the family therapy field toward giving up the stance of knowing for certain what it is that the family requires for therapeutic process, in favor of seeing the family not just as a source of information about their difficulty but as a collaborative therapeutic resource. The object relations approach, based on a collaboration for growth in the matrix of the therapeutic relationship, can be quite useful to the systems family therapist who is ready to stop managing behavior. We encourage the family therapist to develop the capacity to sit back and learn from the ongoing experience rather than having to know things ahead of time and impose things on the family system.

ISN'T THE HERE-AND-NOW EMPHASIS THE SAME AS IN EXPERIENTIAL THERAPY?

Like experiential therapy, object relations theory and therapy value the here-and-now. The difference is that in object relations therapy the here-and-now is connected to its roots in the past. Previous experience is re-created in the here-and-now. In object relations therapy, that connection has to be made. The unconscious influence of previous experience can be made conscious, so that a person can have control over current behaviors and ways of relating.

DO YOU AGREE THAT OBJECT RELATIONS THERAPY IS A FEMINIST APPROACH?

Object relations theory does not speak to issues central to the feminist position, such as poverty, powerlessness, physical abuse, sexual stereotyping, reproductive choice, the glass ceiling on earning, and so on. Object relations therapy does not regard itself as a political process, and the object relations therapist has no agenda more radical than analyzing the blocks to individual freedom. Nevertheless, Deborah Luepnitz regards object relations family therapy as the psychoanalytic method closest to sharing feminist values, because our approach is nonauthoritarian and because we care about women's experience. Object relations theory and therapy fully value men, women, and children, and so they are seen as comprising a fair and mutually facilitative approach that appeals to the feminist family therapist. Our approach does not qualify as feminist, nor is it sexist, on the other hand. We value a humanistic stance equidistant between the sexes, committed equally to male and female development.

Feminist psychologists such as Nancy Chodorow, Carol Gilligan, and Jean Baker Miller point out that Sigmund Freud and Erik Erikson's male-centered view of development as a progression from fusion to autonomy fails to account for female development. Unlike men who value individual agency, women derive self-esteem from their responsiveness to the needs of others and their ability to maintain relationships. From these observations, feminist psychologists conclude that the female self develops in a state of continued dynamic interaction with the mother and significant others. This finding is compatible with the tenets of object relations theory.

According to object relations theory, the self—whether male or female—develops in a relational matrix. There, the self ruthlessly uses the object for its relational needs. The resulting relationship provides the stuff of its being. As the infant matures, the self becomes capable of experiencing concern for the ruthlessly used object and repairing any harm done. The capacity for tending to the other and to the relationship between self and other characterizes the maturing self, whether the infant is male or female.

HOW IS A NONDIRECTIVE METHOD LIKE OBJECT RELATIONS THERAPY COMPATIBLE WITH BEHAVIORAL THERAPY AND, SPECIFICALLY, SEX THERAPY?

We have written extensively about the integration of an object relations therapeutic approach with that of sex therapy grounded in a behavioral format. Object relations therapy can be integrated with other behavioral formats beyond that of sex therapy, but neither of us has had this experience. In sex therapy, the behavioral framework is set up and followed. When impasses occur in progress in the behavioral strategy, the patient or couple is then asked to work associatively in the ordinary psychodynamic way.

Psychodynamic understanding of the object relations history and its relational expression in the marriage is applied to the difficulties in behavioral progression. In practice, sex therapy involves not only a behavioral format of the type originated by William Masters and Virginia Johnson, but also a good deal of education about sexuality. Even this is compatible with a nondirective approach. When education is not sufficient for the couple to keep progressing, analysis of the unconscious factors must occur before learning is possible.

We remain nondirective at the unconscious level even when the format calls for a directive or educational approach at the conscious level. That is to say, we attend to the reaction of the couple or family to our directive interventions. We continue to watch the flow of associations to guide us to underlying unconscious themes. We use our countertransference experience as the clue to the transference being expressed through difficulties in working with us. We then interpret the transference interference to the couple. In this way, we use analytic technique within a behavioral or psychoeducational format.

NOTES

This chapter reviews similarities and differences between object relations theories and other theories, from the psychoanalytic to the behavioral:

Self psychology (Kohut 1971, 1977).
The withdrawn self (Guntrip 1969).
The narcissistic marriage (Lansky 1981, Solomon 1989).
Object relations theory (Kernberg 1976, 1980).
Splitting and repression (Kernberg 1987).
Self and object representation (Jacobson 1965).
Separation-individuation and object relations (Mahler 1968).
Fairbairn's theory and American object relations theory (Masterson 1981).
The individual and the group (Foulkes 1948).
Unconscious assumption groupings and valency (Bion 1959).
Feminist family therapy response to object relations family therapy (Luepnitz 1988).
Feminist psychological views (Chodorow 1978, Gilligan 1982, Miller 1991).
Behavioral sex therapy (Masters and Johnson 1970, Kaplan 1974).

II

Object Relations Theory In Practice

NINE

Principles of
Assessment

Assessment is a complicated, evaluative process that precedes the making of any therapy contract. During the assessment process, patient and consulting therapist review the person's difficulties, develop a tentative object relations formulation, and decide whether therapy is needed or wanted. If treatment is in order, the consulting therapist considers what therapy format to recommend: which modality, which combination of modalities whether serially or concurrently, and which family members wish to be treated. Individual, couple, or family assessment may require only one interview, but more commonly it spans two to four. The assessment process offers the therapist a chance to get to know the patient and it gives the patient a chance to get to know the therapist. The question of fit between patient or patient group and therapist should be considered. Sometimes the individual or family will prefer referral for therapy to a colleague with whom a better fit can be expected. The therapist has not made any commitment to the patient at this point and is freer to be objective in making observations and recommendations. Assessment also operates as a minitrial of therapy that gives the patient a sample of therapeutic process on which to base the decision about future needs for therapy.

WHAT ARE THE FEATURES OF THE ASSESSMENT PROCESS?

The assessment process covers eight major areas.

Table 9–1. The Eight Major Tasks of Assessment
1. Provision of therapeutic space
2. Assessment of developmental phase and level
3. Demonstration of defensive functioning
4. Exploration of unconscious assumptions and under-lying anxiety
5. Working with dreams and fantasies
6. Use of transference and countertransference
7. Testing of response to interpretation and assessment format
8. Making a formulation, recommendation, and treatment plan

1. Provision of therapeutic space

Our main effort goes not into discovering a lot about the patient, but, rather, simply creating an environment that the patient can move into comfortably so that the patient can share private information with the therapist. The patient and therapist join in assessing the patient's psychodynamics, motivation, and therapeutic capabilities.

2. Assessment of developmental phase and level

From the way that the patient relates to us, in the anxious situation of crossing the boundary from life into the consulting room, we can see operating the developmental phase that predominates in the patient's personality and colors the repressed object relationships. For instance, a person who has unresolved issues at the oral level of development may be somewhat clinging or may use words as weapons or as seductive objects upon which to hook the therapist. Someone who has unresolved issues at the anal phase tries to control what the therapist may or may not say, or how the therapist may look or not look at the patient. We may note the showing off and physical display of the patient with issues at the phallic-oedipal level of development.

Stages of psychosexual development

Oral, anal, phallic, and oedipal psychosexual stages of development were described by Freud. He said that they arose according to a predetermined sequence as the drives change their character and the erogenous zone of their expression. Fairbairn preferred to relate the psychosexual stages to techniques of relating. For instance, the family at the oral level relates in a heavily dependent way even when in conflict about such dependency, whereas the patient at the anal stage is more interested in control of the object and access to the object. The individual with oedipal level conflict will trust the therapist and be able to let the therapist go at times of separation, but may fear retaliation from the therapist if the patient competes successfully.

An object relational assessment of phases of development focuses on the patient's capacities for relating.

3. Demonstration of defensive functioning: projective identification

As we work, even in the course of one interview, we will notice some repetitive patterns whereby the patient, couple, or family acts toward therapist or family member in a characteristic way to defend against anxiety expected in the therapeutic situation. We point out the pattern when we first notice it and again when we see it repeated. We try to relate the behavior to the object relations history. We look for ways in which the patient is projecting into the therapist and identifying parts of the self or the objects in the person of the therapist. Then we show the patient that these projective identifications are happening as an attempt to communicate with the other person and as a way of defending against anxiety in the relationship. We find that the interpersonal behavior between patient and therapist, or between members of a family, or between family and therapist, reflects the internal object relations set.

4. Exploration of unconscious patterns, internal object relations, and underlying anxiety

To look for evidence of repressed object relationships, we listen to the clinical material and observe and experience the patient or patient group in relation to ourselves. In the individual session, we review the patient's current and former relationships. If these are not addressed spontaneously, we will remark on the absence of such material and ask for elaboration. We point out recurring patterns that are reported as occurring with significant others and that are directly observable in relation to ourselves and show that these serve a defensive purpose. We then speculate as to what anxiety is being defended against. In therapy with couples and families, we note the interactions among family members and the way that the family deals with us. These interactions tend to occur in a pattern that defends against their shared underlying anxiety and takes form as shared unconscious assumptions about the requirements of family life.

5. Working with dreams and fantasies

We might not expect a spontaneous sharing of dreams and fantasies in assessment, but we certainly always let patients know that this is part of our area of examination. Dream and fantasy material may give access to deeper issues than can be fully addressed during the assessment process. Nevertheless, some work with them lets us begin to assess the unconscious fantasies and internal object constellations that determine conscious behavior without being directly observable, and it gives the patient an opportunity to see what can be done with psychodynamic technique. This use of dreams and fantasies does not stand alone but is interpolated with all the other material to arrive at a first approximation of unconscious organization. This assessment work gives the patient a chance to evaluate the usefulness of therapy.

6. Use of transference and countertransference

We remain alert at all times to the effect that the patient or family is having on us. We monitor our feelings and, from within our own experience, try to make sense of the patient's effect on us and on others in important relationships. We might even make a trial countertransference-based interpretation of the transference during the assessment process.

7. Testing response to interpretation and to the assessment format

When we have made some linking comment or given an interpretation, we watch to see how the patient responds to what we have said. We may have to make further interpretations to help the patient get beyond resistance to the area of interpretation. Other patients will respond quite favorably and use the interpretive work to get to a deeper level. In either case we are interested in how the patients work in the interpretative mode, so as to determine whether object relations therapy is going to be suitable and productive for this patient.

We are also interested in how the patient responds to the frame of the assessment process. Some patients will reveal tendencies to cancel a session, come late or early, renegotiate times, forget to pay fees, object to billing policies, or otherwise attempt to change the conditions that we have established for the assessment process. We work interpretively with these attempts to bend the frame, and we understand their aim is to undo the importance of the assessment intervention and reduce its power. Patients respond to the frame in this way in order to protect themselves from their understandable anxiety about what will be revealed if the assessment process is allowed to proceed in the precise and efficient way originally planned.

8. Making a formulation, recommendation, and treatment plan

From our experience with the patient and information given to us, we make a tentative formulation of the object relations. We decide whether this object relations set requires treatment. If it does, we then recommend to the patient the appropriate level of therapy and the format that is applicable. We might recommend individual psychotherapy, individual psychoanalysis, couple therapy, family therapy, group therapy, group analysis, or any of these in an effective combination. We negotiate this with the patient and when an agreed-upon plan is arrived at, we are then ready to move to a therapeutic contract.

CAN YOU ILLUSTRATE WORK WITH DEFENSE, ANXIETY, COUNTERTRANSFERENCE, AND INTERPRETATION TO DEMONSTRATE THE OBJECT RELATIONS SET OF A COUPLE DURING ASSESSMENT?

This illustration comes from consultation that we did together. It was a two-session assessment for couple therapy with Michelle and Lenny, referred by Lenny's individual therapist. Aspects of this assessment have been described by David Scharff in *Refinding the Object and Reclaiming the Self* and by Jill Scharff in *Clinical Handbook of Marital Therapy*. Michelle and Lenny had been together for four years, but Michelle, an outgoing, social activist had been unable to marry quiet, conservative Lenny because he seemed so passive. A nice, attractive man from an upper-class family more advantaged than her own, successful in business, and loyal to her, he had many appealing qualities. He treated her well, he adored her no matter how she treated him, no matter how fat she allowed herself to get, but she hated his stead-fastness and was full of contempt for his passivity. No way could he meet her expectations. She wanted a man like her amazingly energetic, confident, and admirable brother, whereas the most Lenny offered her was security and devotion. He loved her as much as she hated him. He was steady as a rock, always there, never changing. She was bubbling with energy, rushing along, full of ideas and vivacity. So why was she still with Lenny?

"Because I can't seem to dump the guy. He's a great boyfriend, classiest guy I've ever known," Michelle admitted. "But he is not the kind of man I'm attracted to. With him I'd be trapped in a boring marriage, always lighting a fire under his tush!"

Lenny was not put off by her contempt for him. "I offer her security," he said proudly. "I am a rock, and she's a river running over it. I'll always be there for her. I love everything about her," he affirmed. "The way she speaks, the way she feels. I don't mind her being in the forefront: good protection! She's the world to me."

Provision of therapeutic space

And so they went on, their hectic bantering creating a hilarious routine that made the therapists feel uncomfortably amused, fascinated, and appalled. Even though we were uncomfortable, we had to bear our feelings in order to create an accepting environment where the couple could behave in their usual way and we could be affected by their interaction.

Developmental phase and level

Michelle and Lenny were concerned with issues of holding on and letting go. They are at the developmental phase of formation or dissolution of the ambivalently viewed premarital couple and their developmental mode of relating is at the anal level. Through her overeating, Michelle cannot let go of this unsatisfactory relationship to risk new opportunities, and she holds on to food stores, in case of feelings of deprivation should she let go of Lenny. Lenny sees himself as a rock.

Demonstration of defensive function: projective identification

We showed how Lenny adored Michelle as his mother had adored him. In her, he found a projected, lost part of his ego, while he was identified with his own object. At the same time, Michelle felt that Lenny's passivity was pushing her to be a mother to him, and she adamantly refused to go along with that. It would have re-created for her the envied relationship between her own mother and her brother who had everything. Their projective identificatory system was fashioned from their unconscious communication of their repressed internal object relations seeking expression, confirmation, and modification, but having to be avoided.

Exploration of unconscious patterns, internal object relations, and underlying anxiety

In this case, we demonstrated the defensive pattern of their way of relating and their underlying anxiety by studying their effect on the countertransference, experienced in co-therapy between the co-therapists.

Use of transference and countertransference

I (Jill) made a determined effort to engage with the couple actively and seriously, while my co-therapist (David), who is normally rather energetic, almost fell asleep. Both of these responses reflect our wish to avoid the pain of being with them: mine was closer to the defensive structure of their relationship, whereas David's response was closer to the underlying anxiety. His examination of his countertransference response led to our talking about the underlying sadness in the couple's relationship. Manic defenses had been projected into and identified with by Michelle and me, while the passivity and depression and been projected into and identified with by Lenny and David. The couple's defenses had been split into manic and depressive components, projected into each other. These had now been projected into the co-therapy relationship, and distributed between the co-therapists along gender lines rather than according to the therapists' usual valencies for accepting projections. The therapists were able to discuss their experience in the session and interpreted the defensive projective identificatory system as a defense against the void the couple would face if their destructive bantering were to stop.

Testing the response to interpretation

Immediately the couple responded to our interpretation with a change in the level of affect.

"It's like the jazz bands playing at a funeral," Lenny confirmed, seriously.

Before returning to their defensive position later in the session, the couple was able to explore the void just a little. Lenny's void came from the lack of an active father when he was growing up. Michelle's came from her perception of herself as a girl who did not feel as secure with her mother as her brother did. So she wanted a man like her brother to complete herself, and he wanted a powerful, active woman to replace the adoring, protective mother and sisters he had depended on. Lenny had the woman he wanted, except that Michelle rejected his projective identification of her, whereas she did not have the man she thought she wanted, but instead had someone, enviable like her brother and despicably lacking like herself, with whom to relive her frustration about what she lacked.

Work with dreams and fantasy

This couple did not bring in any dreams. Whereas in individual therapy, a prospective patient already expects the therapist to be interested in dreams, in couple therapy, we have to let the couple know of our interest. We did have access to plenty of unconscious material, including Michelle's fantasy of an ideal man based on the model of her brother. Giving up that incestuous attachment would require work in future therapy.

Further work on developmental phase and level

"Lenny is so average," Michelle complained later in their session. "Average is boring. Whereas I'm special. So why do I hate myself? My mother did that to me. I used to dread being feminine. Now I wouldn't change it for the world. But I was such a tomboy. My brother has that specialness, but he has all the confidence to go with it. A complete winner! And I really envy him because of it. Because I'm missing that little part. There's a part of me that constantly finds holes in herself."

To an analyst, these words speak of penis envy from the phallic stage of development. Usually we address this issue in the broader terms of envy of the man's world. But in this case, both aspects of Michelle's envy were close to consciousness.

"Whatever it is that he has — the confidence that makes him a complete mensch — I'm missing," she added.

"You feel this envy for Lenny, too, as his mother's great little kid," I suggested to Michelle.

But it was Lenny who answered.

"Yes," said Lenny. "In my family, I'm the confident male. In her family, it's her brother. But he's self-confident, cocky. He knows he's good. I'd love to be him, myself."

"Lenny doesn't have that confidence," Michelle continued. "When he's called upon to be a mensch, he can be in certain cases, but not where it counts to me."

"What about where it counts in bed?" I retorted, recalling her feelings about the penis and what it meant to her.

For once Michelle was nonplussed. "You talk about that, dear," she said, yielding the floor to Lenny.

Now we learned that in bed Lenny was the confident sexual partner who had shown great sensitivity to Michelle's vaginismus. He helped her to tolerate intercourse and find sexual release with him. He found her beautiful whether she was fat or thin. For Michelle, who hated her body, Lenny's adoration was both gratifying and contemptible.

"Sex is a pain to me, but I'm as comfortable with Lenny as I can be," Michelle said with resignation. "You know, for a girl who had penis envy as a child, I hate them now. So there's something obviously wrong with me."

"One thing about Lenny you appreciate is that he doesn't force himself on you powerfully in intercourse," I said.

Michelle said, "Right. He's very good to me."

I said, "But as a child, you saw the penis as a source of power."

"I don't remember anything about the penis itself," Michelle corrected me.

I had taken my cue from her use of the words "penis envy." But Michelle had generalized her envy.

"I mean the boy's world," I amended. "The things boys had that you didn't. What I'm saying is that now that you've taken possession of your adult femininity and enjoy a woman's world, it's sad for you that you can't take pleasure from the penis, because you still see it as a source of envied and threatening power."

Michelle said, "I see it as an intrusion! I hate it. I've come a little distance, but I used to see it as a man sticking it to a woman."

I said, "Now you don't *see* it that way, but you still *feel* it like that."

Michelle said, "Not as much as I did before. I used to see it as another way of a man's control, which I hate. But it's never, ever been like that with Lenny."

Making a dynamic formulation

Applying Freudian theory, we can say that as a child, Michelle had thought that a boy like her brother did not feel the ache that she felt for her rejecting mother. She imagined that he did not feel empty as she did because he had the penis that she was missing, while her vagina felt like an empty hole. In her adulthood, the penis continued to be threatening because it could enter that painful hole. That childhood hatred for the penis she now felt toward the man in her adult sexual relationship. The better Lenny did with her sexually, the more she had to attack him enviously. Lenny, though

sexually competent, had some inhibition against being assertive generally and sexually, and he used Michelle as a phallic
front for himself so that he could avoid castration anxiety.
Taking care of her sore vaginal opening reminded him that his
penis was not causing damage and therefore would not be
damaged in retaliation.

In object relations terms, each was using Michelle as a
manic defense against emptiness and sadness. Each was using
Lenny as a depository for the schizoid defense against emptiness. The pain of the void was projected into Michelle's vagina
for which she had a psychophysiological valency, and their
shared longing for healing of the void was focused on attention
to her sexual dysfunction. In therapy they would need to take
back these projective identifications of each other and develop
a holding capacity for bearing their shared anxieties.

Response to assessment format: making a recommendation and treatment plan

The couple's response to the assessment format reflected
their ambivalence about staying together. In their first interview, they worked well with the therapists and seemed to
benefit from the insight they got. But they did not want to
return. Then they called for a second appointment, after
which they again wanted no more contact. When we discussed
the possibility of couple therapy, we were not surprised that
Michelle seemed reluctant: to her it implied a couple commitment that she did not want emphasized. We recommended
that Michelle and Lenny both continue their individual
therapies and that Michelle increase her individual sessions.

How Is the Work that You Do in Assessment Different from Therapy?

It is like therapy, but it is different in that it cannot have quite as free a form as therapeutic sessions that enjoy the luxury of having plenty of time. In assessment, the therapist is sampling the patient's personality rather than experiencing it in its fullness. Nevertheless, assessment involves therapists in an examination of their responses to the task of connecting with the patient at the surface of the personality, which is often just as meaningful and revealing in its own way as the later in-depth engagement when the transference has developed. Another important distinguishing feature is that there is no commitment between patient and therapist. So, if the patient in assessment cancels an appointment, we do not charge for the missed time. During assessment, time is sold on an item-for-service basis rather than for long-term commitment. The significance of the move from assessment to therapy is emphasized by the shift in policy.

Some therapists are more active during the assessment phase than they would be later in therapy. For instance, a therapist may feel that a patient is working well in one area of exploration. This tells the therapist that the person can work in this area, while others are untested. The therapist may tactfully interrupt to point out that other areas are being ignored or may simply inquire about them to complete the picture. For instance, a patient may be talking usefully about family relationships but may avoid the topic of sexual adjustment. In therapy, sexual issues would emerge in due course, but in the assessment phase, it could well be important to ask directly about sexual relating. We do, however, limit the amount of direct questioning, because it interferes with the unconscious flow. The same considerations regarding questioning apply to confrontation or interpretation. The therapist, during the assessment phase, may decide to confront or interpret in order to see how the patient accepts or works with it, while in therapy there is more emphasis on waiting for the right moment to give an interpretation. Nevertheless, we try to follow the patient's associative flow in the assessment process, much as we do in therapy, acknowledging, however, that there will be times when we need to interrupt and broaden our focus in order to get a comprehensive assessment.

WHAT IS THE ROLE OF HISTORY-TAKING IN ASSESSMENT?

We do not advise taking a formal history because we find this generates answers to our questions rather than allowing the patient to generate questions for therapy. We prefer to ask questions about history at moments when that history is alive in the room, for example, at a moment of affect when the patient is talking about a current relationship. We suspect that the current relationship carries a charge from an earlier relationship. We find that this is an advantageous moment to introduce that question.

DO YOU USE GENOGRAMS?

Some psychoanalytic marital therapists, such as Dare, do use genograms. We, however, do not use genograms. As with formal histories, we find that genograms generate information out of context. A person who has a lot of experience taking genograms may make good use of this way of getting the wider picture, but we have found it better to work with affect and transference to generate the information about transgenerational transmission.

On the other hand, during an assessment and usually in the first interview, we generally ask about the relationship to parents and the family of origin, if the information has not emerged spontaneously. Here we are not looking for a comprehensive history but simply for a description of parents as individuals and as a couple and of the patient's fit in the family. During the course of therapy, we would ask about the relationship of an event in current life to experience with parents, specifically after working on its reverberation in the transference, when meaningful internal object information will be linked to healing.

DO YOU ANSWER DIRECT QUESTIONS FROM THE PATIENT DURING THE ASSESSMENT PROCESS?

Questions relative to the management of the therapy should always be answered. For instance, "Will you accept my insurance? What is your fee and billing practice? When do you take your vacations?" At the same time one bears in mind any unconscious significance that these issues might have for the patient. Another question that must routinely be answered pertains to the therapist's professional training and qualifications. While personal questions about marital status, children, religious or political affiliation will not be answered, questions about previous clinical experience and professional background and training call for an open response. Patients have a right to know the qualifications of the therapists to whom they will be making commitment. Any request for consultation from a colleague should be honored and facilitated. Patients have a right to a second opinion, particularly in the consultative phase. And they also have a right to shop around to get the therapist best suited to their needs. We may regret the added stress on us that we face by meeting with a patient who may choose to reject us and work with someone else. Nevertheless, it is in the best interest of the patient and the ensuing therapy that we cooperate with this process.

While all these questions and issues receive a forthright answer, at the same time the therapist wants to bear in mind their reflection of the patient's unconscious issues. Maintaining the balance of considering and perhaps interpreting the unconscious issues while addressing the practical matters openly is, of course, a delicate matter.

How Do You Make a Diagnosis for Third-party Payers?

The requirements of the insurance companies and other interested third parties have to be met, when that is the patient's wish — which it usually must be for economic reasons. We cooperate fully in meeting these requirements and at the same time discuss them openly with the patient. If a diagnosis must be written down, we usually discuss the choice and its implications with the patient.

When we make an object relations assessment of the patient, we come up with a psychoanalytic formulation that we do not share with the third-party payer. To some extent we put on a different hat in order to arrive at the diagnosis that fits the *DSM-III-R* requirements. Working with the patient to review the symptomatology, we choose a relevant diagnosis that will justify the patient's treatment needs and warrant reimbursement.

Like all therapists, we regret the invasion of privacy that managed care and insurance reimbursement introduce into the therapeutic process. We share with patients their concern, in this age of computer theft, that their material will not be kept confidential from employers and future employers. So we discuss with patients the risks and arrive at a suitable adjustment to the realities.

HOW DO YOU HANDLE PEER REVIEW?

Many of these same issues apply to peer review, which may occur at the point of assessment or later on. Here, every effort must be taken to ensure confidentiality and privacy for the patient. Sometimes, a longer narrative report of the psychodynamics and personal issues is requested. Such information must be separated from the patient's actual identity and submitted in an appropriately anonymous way. All of this must be discussed with the patient for protection of the patient's privacy and for the legal protection of the therapist.

WHAT DO YOU MEAN BY ESTABLISHING A FRAME FOR TREATMENT DURING THE ASSESSMENT PROCESS?

At the end of the assessment process, we establish a treatment plan. Within this plan, there is a format in which the treatment will take place. By format, we refer to the plan for, let's say, twice-weekly individual therapy, once-a-week couple therapy, or an agreed-on combination of therapies. Once the plan is set, we stick to it. We establish a fee, how the fee will be paid, a time by which the fee will be paid, and a series of meeting times that will be regularly kept. We start and end the appointment on time. In this way the therapist demonstrates the clarity of the boundaries of the therapeutic space.

It is important to establish a clear frame at the outset so that both patient and therapist understand the initial conditions for establishing therapy. Then we are in a position to examine deviations from the frame. This does not mean that a plan may not be changed later on. But it should be changed by discussion and design rather than by "accidental" infringements brought about by the patient's unconscious acting out. Similarly, of course, we expect that the therapist will not infringe on the frame either. When the therapist fails to hold the frame, she undermines its usefulness as a fruitful stage of examination and makes it hard to encourage the patient to examine and learn from infringements on the frame.

NOTES

The task of assessment is to create an environment for personalized exploration that takes account of the short time frame and limited focus and yet is sufficiently open-ended to give a fair sample of the work of any future therapy:

Psychosexual stages (Freud 1905).

Analytic family therapist's use of the genogram (Dare 1986).

This chapter is mainly a clinical introduction to principles that are addressed and referenced in the next chapter.

TEN

The Technique of Object Relations Therapy: Setting the Frame, Impartiality, Psychological Space, and the Use of the Therapist's Self

WHAT ARE THE MAJOR ASPECTS OF TECHNIQUE?

In the opening phase, we are most concerned with setting the frame, maintaining a neutral position of involved impartiality, and creating a psychological space in which the transference can be expressed and experienced in the countertransference, where the work will begin.

Table 10–1. Elements of Technique of Object Relations Therapy
1. Setting the frame
2. Maintaining a position of neutral, involved impartiality
3. Creating a psychological space for work
4. Using the therapist's self
5. Using transference and countertransference
6. Working with dream and fantasy
7. Interpreting defense, anxiety, and inner object relations
8. Working through
9. Termination

WHAT DOES THE FRAME ENCOMPASS?

Robert Langs described the need for a frame, consisting of psychological boundaries and agreed conditions under which therapy will take place. John Zinner emphasized the use of the flexible frame in family therapy. At the administrative level, the frame consists of the meeting times, the length of the meetings, the usual way of working, who will attend, fees, cancellation policy, and regularity of attendance. Once this is done, patient and therapist have made a commitment to an openly agreed-upon, acceptable framework in which to proceed. Nevertheless, the frame is not to be rigid. It remains flexible to suit changing needs and goals and can be modified by mutual agreement of patient and therapist.

Patients will often try to modify the frame without agreement by the therapist. The frame of the therapy itself becomes the stage for reenactments of the patient's inner object world, as repressed object relationships seek expression in relationship to the therapist. It is, therefore, important that the frame not be bent without thought by patient or therapist and that attacks on the shape of the therapeutic frame be understood as enactments. This is different from the modification of the frame, that is, the frame kept flexible by mutual agreement as the therapist and patient think through changing needs as they are revealed during the course of the therapy.

WHAT IS RESISTANCE?

During therapy patients often express excuses as to why it is impossible to attend sessions, why they come late, and why they should not discuss certain topics. These behaviors are manifestations of resistance. *Resistance* is the term for the patient's effort to repress painful feelings and fantasies and keep them in the unconscious. An analysis of why patients need to defend themselves in these individually significant ways is known as *defense analysis*. Understanding fantasies of shame, embarrassment, or guilt should enable patients to feel more comfortable in revealing the repressed material. Working toward de-repression requires tact and firmness at the same time.

Harry Guntrip described a number of major sources of resistance. He said that resistance occurs when the adult part of the patient feels ashamed when experiencing the child part of the self in relation to the therapist. Resistance occurs to defend the existence of the self. The main source of resistance to therapy is the tenacity with which we hold on to our libidinal attachments to our parents, no matter how troubled our actual relationships with them may have been. At first, patients long for their therapists to rescue them from their parents. Then they become afraid that they will meet their parents again in the person of the therapist. Lastly, when change seems possible, they fear that the therapist will rob them of their internal parents and expose them to the underlying void.

HOW IS THERAPY ESTABLISHED?

In the beginning phase of therapy, the therapist wants to listen to and learn from and about the patient. Rather than a barrage of questions, the therapist's enquiring attitude encourages the patient to reveal the problems that require therapy and the nature of the patient's life, relationships, and inner conflicts. The therapist attends to conscious and unconscious material. We remain neutral as to what we find out. We are empathic, but not sympathetic, to the patient's basic needs. In this phase, as in other phases, we follow the patient's lead while noting our own internal responses, without necessarily doing or saying anything about them.

The therapist does take the lead, however, in providing the way of working. This means asking some questions about affective connections between current conflicts and past conflicts, and understanding the importance of current relationships and their connection to the object relations history.

HOW DO YOU TAKE AN OBJECT RELATIONS HISTORY?

Some therapists stress an exhaustive history as an important part of an initial evaluation. In object relations therapy we, too, are interested in those aspects of a patient's past that illuminate the current conflict. Rather than trying to get an exhaustive developmental or relational history, however, we are more interested in asking an open-ended question, such as, "What was it like for you in some earlier phase of your life?" For instance, when a couple comes with a marital conflict, we might ask what it was like for them to be growing up with their own parents and how were their parents' marriages experienced by each of them in childhood. Thus the history that we get relates to the internal object relations as they are expressed currently in everyday relationships and self-experience. We limit the ambition of our history-taking, because we have found that a more exhaustive history may give us ideas, but is at such a distance from the patient's current emotional life as not to be particularly useful. We prefer to gather gradually a history of earlier relationships brought to mind at moments of affective intensity or impasse in the course of therapy, rather than getting an early catalog that will probably not be remembered by either the patient or the therapist.

HOW CAN YOU ENLARGE THE AREA OF OBJECT RELATIONS UNDERSTANDING?

In individual therapy, we encourage the patient to tell us more by our attitude of interest and by asking questions or making observations related to what the patient has already told us. As patients give us more pieces of information, we see links between them. Together, we work to understand more. For instance, if a patient has told us about a current conflict and then about a period of conflict during an earlier developmental period, we might ask how those two periods of time are similar or different. We might ask if there have been echoes in earlier adult developmental phases, or in the lives of members of the previous generation, especially the parents. We also suggest affective links between episodes as they occur to us and wait for the patient to confirm or modify our hypotheses. Gradually we get an enlarged picture of the patients' external lives, their internal object relationships, and the links between these.

In couple and family therapy, we enlarge the field of observation by asking for the perspectives of all those present and giving each person a chance to speak. This has the same standing as asking individual patients to describe aspects of their lives from several points of view. Observations of all the participants in the room develop this shared family or marital view.

HOW DO YOU CREATE A PSYCHOLOGICAL SPACE?

In these ways, we use the safety of the therapeutic environment to create a psychological space inside us and between ourselves and the patient. This space that communicates between self and other is comparable to Winnicott's "potential space." Into this space, aspects of the patient's internal and external worlds are brought for examination. Therapist and patient experience and observe their impact on each other and on the relationship between them. They play in the gap between patient and therapist to create new ways of perceiving and relating.

WHAT ABOUT USING THE HERE-AND-NOW VERSUS THERE-AND-THEN?

We especially value what we have called the *core affective exchange*. This occurs between patient and therapist, or in the conjoint therapies, among family members or between family and therapist, at an emotionally intense moment. This means that internal object relationships are alive in the here-and-now of the room, brought into the session in a full and immediate way. Experiencing these exchanges in the here-and-now gives us a more powerful way of understanding the individual, and couple or family relationships, than when experiences are reported as having occurred at some other time and place.

WHAT DO YOU MEAN BY THE TERM *INVOLVED IMPARTIALITY?*

We apply Helm Stierlin's term *involved impartiality* to refer to our therapeutic attitude. We maintain a position, neutral as to symptomatology, goals, direction of the therapeutic process, and outcome. We remain equidistant between the conscious and unconscious parts of the patient's personality and equidistant in our temporary identification between self and object and between the various generations represented in the functioning of the internal object relationships affecting the transference. With previous experience and therapy, we prepare ourselves as ground for object relating in which patients can discover themselves and grow. In other words, we make ourselves available for use as just the kind of object that the patient requires us to be in order for the patient to find him- or herself.

WHAT IS NEGATIVE CAPABILITY?

We also develop a capacity to be uncertain and to not have to know exactly what is going on while we explore unknown, unformed, and anxious areas. This capacity has been called *negative capability,* a phrase that derives from Keats' description of Shakespeare's poetic capacity for "being in uncertainties, mysteries and doubts without irritable reaching after fact and reason." Wilfred Bion applied this technique to his therapeutic stance. He encouraged therapists to be "without memory or desire" in relation to the patient. Christopher Bollas writes that it is the therapist's task to help the patient give form to the "unthought known," aspects of the self that are but that have not been recognized in thoughts and words. We do not put words on them: we interpret the patient's blocks against knowing and thinking, so that the patient can rediscover lost parts of the self and teach us about them. We want to know no more than the patient does. We do not want our own therapeutic ambition to block the patient's search.

The therapist allows the therapeutic task to emerge from the patient, just as the mother allows her baby to explore. The mother needs to have an ideal of maturation and growth in mind, but she does not impose a form on it that would violate the baby's need to develop its self. This paradox of knowing and not knowing, of form and formlessness, is at the heart of therapy. Therapists can have their own values about growth, development, and maturation, but they prefer not to impose their own images of the improved patient, since this destroys the patient's self-discovery of what Bollas calls "the personal idiom."

At the same time "being without memory or desire" does not mean that the therapist is not to know anything. We do form hypotheses about the patient's conflicts and difficulties. These get tried out by being given as interpretations to the patient, who then works with them, provides corrections, confirmations, or the conclusion that certain hypotheses do not fit with the patient's organization at all.

CAN YOU PROVIDE AN EXAMPLE FROM THE OPENING PHASE OF INDIVIDUAL THERAPY?

Mrs. Epstein (referred to again in Chapter 14) originally consulted me (JSS) about her anxious 11-year-old daughter, with whom she had a conflicted relationship. The relationship was exhausting and left Mrs. Epstein feeling fatigued, tearful, defeated, and "low as a skunk." It was important to Mrs. Epstein to be a good and loving person, and so it was terrible for her to feel that her daughter did not love her. She overfunctioned to take good care of her child.

She was uncomfortably aware of her intense fears of something bad happening to the girl, and she had to engage in many obsessional rituals to prevent her fears from coming true. She could not admit to her underlying rage at her child. She was also unable to ask for therapy for herself.

The flexible frame

The frame of our working arrangement was that of a consultation with family interviews and individual interviews for Mrs. Epstein and for her child. This frame was impinged upon when Mrs. Epstein telephoned to ask for additional sessions for herself. I did not arrange these, but asked her to discuss her request in the next family meeting. Her husband, who had been aware of her depression and obsessions, was relieved that Mrs. Epstein wanted to talk to me, and a change in the frame was agreed. The consultation would be extended over a few more weeks, with two sessions a week for Mrs. Epstein, while her child completed psychometric and educational testing with a colleague, prior to the final interpretive session in which I would make my recommendations to them.

Object relations history

In her individual extended assessment sessions, Mrs. Epstein linked her worry about her child to her own traumatic loss of her mother at the age of 12. She had adored her mother and was devastated by her sudden death in a car crash. During the assessment phase, Mrs. Epstein also idealized me. Much later in subsequent treatment, she began to experience me as a remote and uncaring object, in a re-edition of her experience with a sad, withdrawn mother and a neglectful father.

Working with defense and anxiety about destructiveness

Destructive wishes against her child (who stood both for her own bad self that might have caused her mother's death and for the mother who abandoned her) were being defended against by fear. After we had worked on this defense against destructive urges, Mrs. Epstein could discover and admit to her own impulses to harm her daughter. Mrs. Epstein now realized that she was depressed and needed help for herself more urgently than for her child, but she resisted making a commitment to therapy.

Working with resistance

My first task was to create a safe environment in which Mrs. Epstein felt that her needs would be taken into account, as well as those of others in the family. She needed time to assess my commitment to her before she dared to open up to me. Reassured by my neutral attitude that I would neither judge her nor reject her for her neediness and badness and that I would not drop dead in response to what she told me about her nasty self, Mrs. Epstein became able to confront her resistance to analysis, the form of treatment that she herself thought was her last hope. She was afraid to lie down because she might experience a strong urge to go to sleep. Associations to a dream made it clear that she wished for and feared a deep sleep in which she could join her mother in peaceful union. After analyzing this fantasy, Mrs. Epstein told me that she now felt able to lie on the couch and make a commitment to treatment, but only if I could be her analyst.

Impartiality

Some years before, a transfer from a trusted therapist to an analyst had been disastrous for her, and she could not face that again. Since the child had not catapulted herself into a transference relationship with me, I agreed with Mr. and Mrs. Epstein that it would be best to refer the child to a colleague for individual therapy while Mrs. Epstein would have analysis with me. It could be argued that I did not remain equally partial to all family members in this case, because I chose to work with the mother, not the presenting patient. But I think that I made my recommendation from a position of involved impartiality to the needs of the whole family. This facilitated the emergence of the mother's individual needs, and she was ultimately more able to be helpful to her daughter.

Use of the here-and-now, transference–countertransference, and negative capability

Mrs. Epstein had been talking about her wonderful mother, about whom she had the fondest feelings. According to her memory, they had never been angry at each other. Her mother was a vital, engaging woman who had never been sick until the day she died. A month after Mrs. Epstein began analysis, I caught a severe cold. Mrs. Epstein became silent every time I coughed. I could not understand why I felt so ill from just a cold. Perhaps the cold virus was particularly virulent, but more likely the infection was moving into my chest because, in the countertransference, I felt compelled not to cough. Although I dutifully attended to the patient's material, I could not listen freely and respond cognitively or emotionally, because I was anxiously inhibiting any changes in my breathing that might trigger another cough, lest I aggravate her dread of my fate.

What was this doing to my state of negative capability? I was certainly not without memory or desire. I kept remembering Mrs. Epstein's frozen reaction to my coughing. I was full of the desire to stop coughing and to have the patient go away and leave me alone. My state of negative capability was being impinged on by my own concerns. On the other hand, meaning was about to emerge from this experience.

I felt quite sick. I needed to be able to cough and get rid of this infection and its interference with my state of freely suspended attention and negative capability; so I took the next day off to recover. Mrs. Epstein was unnerved. She could not contain her anxiety. She yelled at her children, then spent a sleepless night worrying about whether they would die. I recognized this as an early transference manifestation. Mrs. Epstein had experienced me as her mother suddenly being absent. Her rage at me was not expressed directly, but was displaced onto her child, as was her rage at her mother. Sobbing guiltily, Mrs. Epstein told me that she thought that she had caused my illness by her failure: if she had been a more loving person, this illness would not have happened to me. From the here-and-now of the therapeutic relationship experienced in the transference as fear of loss and guilt at causing my illness and felt in the countertransference as a worsening of my physical condition, we moved to a preliminary reconstruction of Mrs. Epstein's guilt about her mother's death. We would return to this many times in the course of therapy, each time understanding more about her fantasy of having killed her mother.

DO YOU USE THE IDEAS OF *IMPARTIALITY* AND *NEGATIVE CAPABILITY* INSTEAD OF THE ANALYTIC CONCEPT OF *ABSTINENCE?*

No. Impartiality and negative capability are aspects of the therapist's technique that are developed in addition to Freud's basic condition of abstinence. Freud advised the therapist to abstain from seeking gratification from the patient. This means that we do not entertain personal, social, or sexual relationships with patients, because we are dedicated to putting aside our own interests in receiving pleasure from the patient in order to clear ourselves for use as the necessary object in fantasy. It also means that we do not gratify the patient's wishes, but rather seek to understand them. For instance, in intensive therapy we generally do not respond with a direct answer to questions or give advice, so that we do not undermine our task of uncovering and exploration. On the other hand, abstinence does not require being rude and rejecting to patients. For us, abstinence refers to our intention to remain in the work mode of the central ego, available for use as whatever object we are required to be in fantasy, but in reality not introducing ourselves as either exciting or rejecting objects. In practice, this means that we behave naturally, but professionally, supporting the expression of whatever wishes the patient struggles with, but not gratifying them. Through abstinence, we ensure that we do not smother, undo, make up for, or obliterate painful desires.

DO YOU MEAN THAT YOU NEVER GIVE SUPPORT AND ADVICE?

There is some room in object relations therapy for support and advice, but they do not form the heart of our method. It is not that support and advice are against the rules; they are simply not the work horses of object relations therapy. In supportive psycho-therapy or in parent guidance, giving advice has a greater role than in a more ambitious therapy, in which exploring unknown terri-tory and interpreting what is learned will be more important. There is nothing more truly supportive than an accurate, correctly timed interpretation.

NOTES

After listing the major aspects of technique of object relations therapy, we describe and illustrate how to create a firm, safe, but flexible therapeutic space in which to work psychologically with defense, resistance, and anxiety toward object relations understanding. Most important is the use of the therapist's self, in particular the ability for involved impartiality and negative capability:

The frame of treatment (Langs 1976, Zinner 1985).
Resistance as a defense (Guntrip 1969).
Potential space (Winnicott 1951).
Core affective exchange (Scharff and Scharff 1987).
Involved impartiality (Stierlin 1977).
Keats's term "negative capability" (Murray 1955, p. 261).
Without memory and desire (Bion 1970).
The unthought known, personal idiom (Bollas 1987, 1989b).
Abstinence (Freud 1915b).
Interpretation (Strachey 1934, Stewart 1990).

ELEVEN

The Technique of Object Relations Therapy: Working with Transference, Countertransference, and Interpretation

Developing negative capability and maintaining abstinence and impartiality enable us to respond to the patient's transference. In studying our reactions to the unconscious material in individual, couple, or family therapy, we find that countertransference experiences that are evoked by patients' transferences tend to cluster into two groups. We have called these the contextual and the focused countertransferences. The *contextual countertransference* refers to the therapist's reaction to the patient's *contextual transference*. The *focused countertransference* refers to the therapist's reaction to the patient's *focused transference*.

Contextual transference is the patient's reaction to the therapeutic space that we have provided, corresponding to the care offered by the "environment mother." The patient reveals this transference in attitudes about the frame of treatment in conscious feelings and behavior toward the therapist as the provider of the therapeutic environment.

The *focused transference* refers to feelings that the patient displaces onto the therapist as an object for intimate relating, corresponding to the "object mother" in relation to the infant self. This early relationship can be re-created in the transference in two ways that were pointed out by Racker from his study of the therapist's countertransference to them. He noted that the countertransference arose from a state of concordant or complementary identification. Where the therapist is identified with a projected part of the object, we call this a *complementary identification*. Conversely, sometimes the patient identifies with the object mother and experiences the therapist as a part of the self in relation to that object. Where the therapist is identified with a part of the patient's ego, we call this a *concordant identification*.

Most of what has been written about transference in psychodynamic therapy refers to the focused transference. In this aspect of transference, the therapist becomes a discrete object fashioned according to the requirements of the patient's internal object relationships, or a part of the patient's ego in relation to a discrete object. This aspect of transference develops only after a long time has elapsed in therapy, and especially in psychoanalysis. The earlier and therefore more common form of transference is the contextual transference. In a positive contextual transference, the patient expects the therapist to be benign and facilitating. In a negative contextual transference, the patient expects that the therapist will interfere or be destructive. In response to a positive contextual transference, the therapist feels trusted and potentially helpful. When there is a negative, rejecting contextual transference, the therapist is apt to feel abused, ignored, or mistrusted. In response to an excited form of a negative contextual transference, the therapist may feel excited, aroused and endangered, seduced, suffocated, or drained. The transference is diagnosed from review of its effect on the therapist.

CAN YOU PROVIDE AN EXAMPLE
OF FOCUSED AND CONTEXTUAL
TRANSFERENCE AND
CONCORDANT AND
COMPLEMENTARY
COUNTERTRANSFERENCE IN
INDIVIDUAL THERAPY?

Ms. Harvey (also reported in *Object Relations Family Therapy,* Chapter 10) a single, 32-year-old graphics artist, in the mid-phase of individual psychoanalytic psychotherapy, began her therapy session with a challenge to me (DES):

"Say something! Don't you know this is no way to do this with me? You're so stubborn."

When I tried to ask her a question about her feelings, she yelled at me, "No, that's not it. You just interrupted me again. You never ask at the right time."

I said that I felt silenced, and, although I knew that Ms. Harvey could not always answer such questions, I asked what this reminded her of from her early life.

She said testily, "You know goddamned well it's my mother. So what else?"

"But you've told me before that you didn't yell like this as a child."

"No, I never yelled," she agreed. "I couldn't even speak! But *she* yelled at me, and I just felt worse and worse."

So, Ms. Harvey was acting like her mother and treating me the way she had felt treated as a child. Our task was to understand the reason she had to act this way now.

In this example, the patient complains about the contextual transference, but in fact she works openly and trustingly within it, an improvement since the early part of her treatment, when she was too fearful of the therapeutic relationship to allow this kind of material to emerge. At that time, her *contextual transference* to the contextual holding provided by the analyst was pervaded by distrust derived from her early experience, but interpretive work and experience of a reliable therapeutic holding environment permitted the development of a sufficiently secure contextual transference. With that in place, she could now convey the substance of her core relationship in the *focused transference* by projecting into the therapist a part of herself while she acted like the persecuting internal part-object of her mother.

A few weeks later, Ms. Harvey began with her recurrent refrain, "I'm too tired to talk today. I've been up all night on a project deadline and if you want me to do anything here, you are going to have to ask me the questions. You know I don't agree with the way you try to get me to talk."

I felt annoyed, with a "here-we-go-again feeling." But I wanted to be helpful and decided to ask if anything occurred to her about the situation of being questioned.

"That's not the right question, you dolt!" she retorted. "I've told you and told you that if you want me to tell you anything, you have to ask me specific things." She continued to rail against me in similar vein.

Eventually Ms. Harvey told me about a situation at work where her boss had asked people in detail about their projects. Ms. Harvey had felt dumb and speechless. She was so mad at him for "quizzing her" that she wanted to be able to yell questions back at him and grill him.

I realized that I had been feeling grilled and harassed in the first part of the hour, and that Ms. Harvey was far angrier than she had been earlier in the analysis. This helped me to realize that I was being treated as the patient felt treated, and I now realized that I often felt "abused" by her in this way. I tended to get pulled into a fight with Ms. Harvey, a way of working that left me feeling contentious and dissatisfied with myself. After a few moments, I would grow silent, only to be dragged back into the ring by Ms. Harvey's demand. "Where are you? I need for you to ask me a question. What do you think about what I have just said?"

Working with my feeling badgered and dissatisfied, I asked, "When I don't answer your question the right way, who do I remind you of?"

This time Ms. Harvey responded, "The person you're acting like is *me!* And I'm acting like everybody else: my sister, mother, teachers I've hated as a teenager, my ex-husband. I would never fight. When they asked me questions, and I got confused, I would get silent. I would tell myself that the thing to do was to not get in a fight. But I wanted to yell!"

"My mother used to sit me in a chair and try to teach me to read. And she'd yell at me if I got words wrong. She'd say, 'You're not performing up to your potential. You'll never amount to anything if you keep going like this.' And she'd be screaming at me. I was 5 years old, for Christ's sake! I'd get so quiet, and she would shout, 'Don't sit there! You better talk or else!' And I'd want to yell at *her,* just so she'd know how it felt, what she was doing to me."

I now felt relieved. I no longer felt taken over by a strange and unlikeable part of myself, badgered into a contentious silence. I felt more relaxed, more like myself again.

Ms. Harvey had taken back a painful part of her own internal experience.

In the same hour, Ms. Harvey now went on to tell me about her new relationship with a man with whom she felt more trusting and loving than before. It was so different from her marriage. She was able to relate her attack on me to her feeling that I did not have confidence in this new relationship. She noted that she was now ready to admit that if I had been suspicious that her previous relationships with lovers were not mature, I would have been right, but that previously she did not trust me enough to admit it. In fact, she would insist that they were mature even while knowing that if I saw her with these men, I would have been dubious right away.

"I never could have told you that before," she admitted. "You know, I can only yell at you like I have been, because I trust you. And I've never trusted anyone enough to yell at them, no matter how angry or upset I felt. And then I can also tell you about this new relationship. I do appreciate it that you've forced me to keep going tonight although I was tired. You've been a prod to me, keeping me going."

The word "prod" resonated for me, I realized that that was a function I felt made to perform, with the implication of punishing, teasing, or goading the patient in a pseudo-phallic way.

I was projectively identified with the patient's ego, while she was identified with her persecuting maternal object. My asking her about the origins of this role relationship was like the "prodding" that the patient experienced with her mother. After this work by the patient, I felt relieved of the projective identification, or *focused transference* from her persecuting object, which had partly taken me over. When she trusted me in the *contextual transference* enough to tell me about her new relationship, I felt restored to being a benign object for the patient. From this more secure position, she confirmed her previous lack of trust in the contextual transference earlier in the analysis.

To understand the contextual transference, I had to tolerate feeling attacked and badly treated. Ms. Harvey repeatedly attacked my ability to contain the work. But, as she made clear in this hour, her ability to attack me now represented a newfound capacity for a trusting contextual transference, an ability that she had given up early in her life, or perhaps never had at all. My overall capacity to contain her anxious assaults eventually gave the patient faith in being held safely in my mind. This vignette demonstrates conviction in the strengthened container that allows the focused transference and countertransference to grow and the work on understanding them to proceed.

Later in treatment, within a confident contextual transference, the focused transference became more intense. In contrast to the earlier example in which I was identified with part of her self and she was identified with her own persecuting object, this time the transference was to me as her object, while Ms. Harvey was now identified with her self. Ms. Harvey became extremely vulnerable to experiencing me as an abandoning object when my vacations approached.

A few weeks before the summer, Ms. Harvey became suicidal. She immediately found another new relationship, recovered her hold on life, and assured me that because of her new man, everything was fine. When I suggested that the relationship and the speed of its formation might have defensive functions to ward off her fear of depending on me when I was soon to be away, she became furious. She scratched her head in disbelief and dismay, and said in twenty different ways that I seemed not to be able to understand anything at all.

"Shut up! It doesn't matter whether you understand or not," she concluded.

When she left at the end of the hour, she straightened her hair and said, "I'm sorry for being such a bitch. I know I have to do it, but I'm sorry you have to put up with it!"

The next day she came in and said, "It's not easy to say this. As soon as I got to my car I knew you were right. I think I have been mad at you for going on vacation. You are like my father deserting me, and I can't stand to have you leave when I need you so much. And I can't stand to say it to you. I mean I can now, but it's still not easy."

The *focused transference* is contained and modified in therapy by the therapist's willingness to be experienced as projected parts of the patient's ego and objects while at the same time being his own less harsh self. The patient moves from a *projective identification,* in which the therapist is felt to be the patient's antilibidinal object, to an *introjective identification* with that modified projective identification after it has been detoxified by its journey through the therapist-container. In addition, the patient grows through introjective identification of the therapist's containing function and better-metabolized internal object relations.

CAN A FOCUSED TRANSFERENCE BE SUBSTITUTED FOR A CONTEXTUAL TRANSFERENCE?

Some patients impose a premature focused transference on the therapeutic situation. Frequently in the diagnostic category of borderline or hysteric, these patients will attempt to recruit their therapists as immediate replicas of critical or excited figures from their life. Fearing that the therapist will not be able to hold firm as a facilitating environmental figure, the patient substitutes for the neutral therapist an erotic, aggressive, or other similarly distorted object to compensate for the missing environmental object of the patient's internal world. Interpretation of this phenomenon is required early in such a therapy in order to address the patient's fear that therapy will not provide a safe holding environment.

HOW IMPORTANT ARE TRANSFERENCE AND COUNTERTRANSFERENCE?

Transference and countertransference are central to the technique of object relations therapy. They provide a workable, current version of the patient's object relations as lived out in the relationship with the therapist. This forms the laboratory in the here-and-now, where the internal object relations can be felt and lived out and thereby understood — rather than simply talked about intellectually.

IS TRANSFERENCE THE SAME AS PROJECTIVE IDENTIFICATION?

In the classical sense, no. In Freud's terms, transference referred to the displacement of impulses onto the person of the therapist as their new target. In object relations terms, transference is the same as projective identification. The therapist is identified with a part of the object or a part of the self that has been projected into him, and the internal object relationship is then re-created between the patient and the therapist, where it can be reworked.

WHAT IS THE ROLE OF INTERPRETATION IN OBJECT RELATIONS THERAPY?

From James Strachey, an early Freudian who knew object relations theory, to Harold Stewart, a contemporary analyst in the British Independent group, analysts have used the word *interpretation* to refer to a continuum of therapist interventions, from complex formulations that are mutative to simple comments, on the way to building shared understanding. The therapist gathers observations — including the patient's own observations — feeds them back to see if the patient agrees with them, and links or clarifies things that have been diffusely presented but not clearly understood by the patient. The patient is given the chance to object to or modify what the therapist has said, partly to respect the patient's need for defense and partly to have the patient fine-tune the interpretation. With experience and in supervision, we learn when to take a patient's correction of an interpretation at face value and when to take it as a disavowal. We generally find that an overly energetic response, such as Ms. Harvey's "Shut up!" is more likely to be denial than a thoughtfully suggested modification. We take the patient's reactions fully into account in continuing to modify our own understanding.

Interpretation begins with linking and clarifying and proceeds all the way to understanding how whatever happened long ago in the patient's life influences current difficulties in relationships. The most effective interpretation begins with the current reenactment in the transference and countertransference and proceeds to the reconstruction of repressed internal object relationships.

NOTES

Relevant work includes:
  The focused transference and countertransference, the contextual transference and countertransference (Scharff and Scharff 1987).
  Complementary and concordant transference identification (Racker 1968).
  Transference (Freud 1905a).

TWELVE

Technique: The Use of Dream, Fantasy, and Play In Object Relations Therapy

HOW IS THE DREAM USED IN OBJECT RELATIONS THERAPY?

Freud said that dreams were the royal road to the unconscious. Dreams enable the patient to get to a level far beyond conscious understanding. When the patient brings a dream, we listen and wait for associations to the dream in the standard psychoanalytic way. We do not ask questions or look for answers to puzzles in the content of the dream, but we simply record the patient's thoughts that occur in relation to the dream. The therapist, who knows the patient well, may also have thoughts in relation to the dream that may facilitate the patient's coming forth with more material and understanding. The form of the dream reveals the patient's internal object relations. Whether in psycho-analysis or less intensive psychotherapy, the dream is most effectively interpreted, as it reflects the transference.

In family, couple, or group therapy, dreams provide a communication in the interpersonal field. Here the dream is first understood by the dreamer, who gives his own thoughts and may share his understanding of his dream. Then the dream is opened up to associations from all others in the therapeutic setting — spouse, family members, or group members. Their thoughts and associations form part of the field of understanding, not only of the individual dreamer but also of the dream's implications for the entire therapeutic group. The individual's dream is regarded as a communication about the transference from the couple, family, or group.

In Freudian theory, the dream results from the intricate combination of the mind's residue of the day's events with internal fantasy and expresses the fulfillment of an infantile wish. In Fairbairn's object relations theory, the dream reveals intrapsychic structure.

We have described Fairbairn's six-part model of the endopsy-chic situation: a central ego and its ideal object, characterized by reasonable internal harmony; the rejecting object and the internal saboteur (which he later called the antilibidinal ego), characterized by anger, persecutory anxiety, and frustration; and the exciting object and the libidinal ego, characterized by longing and the anxiety of excessively aroused neediness. The internal structures of the ego are capable of generating meaning and action, and they are in constant dynamic relationship with each other. Fairbairn thought that dreams were to be understood not as wishes, but as *statements of internal psychic structure.* He demonstrated the relationship between the elements of the psyche as illustrated in the dreams.

HOW DOES THE DREAM REFLECT THE BEGINNING THERAPEUTIC ALLIANCE, THE CONTEXTUAL TRANSFERENCE, THE INTRAPSYCHIC STRUCTURE, AND THE COUNTERTRANSFERENCE?

Adam, an unemployed 26-year-old engineer, recently remarried, sought treatment for his dependency on women, his fears of sexual inadequacy, and his inability to get a job. This example is elaborated in *Reclaiming the Object and Refinding the Self*. In the middle of his first analytic session with me (DES) when I was a fledgling analyst, Adam reported a dream from the night before:

The Los Angeles Dodgers asked me to play right field because they were a player short. What would the pitchers think of me? How should I bat against them? I tried to keep from dreaming what I would do when at the plate. I said, "Why not wait until you're up at bat?" I worried that I'd drop the ball in right field.

Adam went on to tell me about the resentment he felt toward his father. He said that his father's impatient criticism during baseball instruction from the age of 4 was the reason that Adam had worried about performing sexually. Then he thought of Thomas Mann's *The Magic Mountain* in which the doctor–patient relationship is homosexually consuming and does not cure the patient.

The dream and the beginning therapeutic alliance

The dream conveyed Adam's fears that beginning psychoanalysis would be like learning baseball with his father. It suggested that he wanted me to teach him something, but saw me as threatening and disapproving, like his father.

"He would watch at practice or Little League games and I'd just feel I never played well enough," Adam said. "I remember dropping the ball once in right field to lose a game and I couldn't face him. I was so mad at him for wanting me to do well."

"You were mad at him for wanting you to do well when you felt you couldn't measure up," I said. "You're afraid of that recurring here. I'm like the pitchers: you're worried what I'll think of you, but you are also playing against me, as I throw balls that you have to hit."

"I think you'll be trying to get me out," he corrected me. "Or that you'll be a much better player than I am. After all, this is your sport. You're the one who is supposed to know how to play."

As an inexperienced analyst too eager to let him know that I understood, I quickly responded, "So you're trying not to worry about it, while you wait to see if you can hit the ball. But you're also worried that when I hit the ball to you, you'll drop the ball."

"Yeah, then there's nothing you could do to help me," he said flatly.

"Then it would be like the relationship between the doctor and patient in *The Magic Mountain*," I acknowledged. "Consuming but it won't cure."

The dream as comment on the contextual transference

I felt threatened by the allusion to the homosexual relationship between the doctor and patient, and the question of whether I would be exploitative. I decided to comment on Adam's anxiety about starting treatment, ostensibly for the correct technical reason of securing the treatment. I did not work with the countertransference idea that popped into my head as a question: "What sort of balls will I throw at him?" Deciding that it was too soon to comment on his homosexual fears or wishes, I filed them away for future consideration.

The dream also revealed his resistance to therapy. I interpreted his fear of facing me and his wish to please both me and himself as a transference from his relationship with his father, but in the context of wanting to compete with me and fearing failure by him—and by me. He moved rapidly toward this premature focused transference to me as the opposing pitcher and hitter because he was afraid that I would not be like a benign, well-meaning coach who would support his efforts to grow and compete.

The dream as a display of intrapsychic structure

Adam's dream also revealed his intrapsychic structure. Here was a boyish part of himself—his libidinal object relationship—locked in an intense, self-defeating struggle with the rejecting object relationship, based apparently on his relationship to his father. The possibility of playing and being praised was as elusive as the tantalizing exciting object, and the inevitability of being blamed was the rejecting object. The internal saboteur made him drop the ball. The "one player short" for whom he was substituting refers to the inadequacy of his central ego functioning, as demonstrated in his symptomatology. Being a good team player embodies the ideal object that he does not have. Perhaps the "one player short" also refers to a feeling of deprivation in relation to his feeding mother, a feeling that his father may have shared, hence his extraordinary pressure on his son to gratify him. For whatever reason to be discovered later in treatment, Adam had not come to terms with oedipal defeat gracefully, and so had been unable to compete successfully and aggressively in the world of work. In his intimate life he was not confident of his sexual functioning, and he could not love a woman without recruiting her as a source of support.

Countertransference in work with dreams

Adam's dream not only told us about him, but plumbed the depths of my valency to respond to his self and object projective identifications. In my countertransference to the dream, I felt consciously more identified with Adam (his *self* projective identification) than with his physician-father. Would my efforts be any better than the all-consuming relationship that did not cure? Would I drop the ball? What would my analytic teachers think of me? On the other hand, like his father (his *object* projective identification), I desperately wanted Adam to do well, so that I could do well and make it to the Major Leagues as a fully certified analyst. That was why I had shelved the homosexual reference: I could not face how dependent I felt on Adam for my training. My countertransference reflected the homosexual longing of the doctor in *The Magic Mountain* and at the same time the patient's fears of empty promises about an incurable disease.

As well as revealing intrapsychic structure, dreams convey interpersonal meaning even within the intrapsychic focus of individual therapy or psychoanalysis. The telling of a dream in psychoanalysis or individual therapy is an interpersonal communication. Dreams join in the conversation of the therapy and express the issues between therapist and patient, sometimes expressing the resistance of the dreamer, sometimes portraying the transference, other times heralding a shift in psychic structure.

HOW DO WE USE FANTASIES IN OBJECT RELATIONS THERAPY?

Fantasies are dealt with like dreams. We hear the fantasy, observe the associated affect, and wait for the flow of associations. We note that a fantasy that may seem to be a private expression of the intrapsychic realm also has its expression in current object relationships.

Working with fantasy and inner object relations in the mid-phase of couple therapy

Dr. Arthur and Mrs. Rhonda Clark (more fully described in *Object Relations Couple Therapy,* Chapter 6) had been working with me (JSS) for a year. We had worked on Arthur's passivity, his inability to earn Rhonda's admiration of him as a successful, ambitious, caring man, and his need to denigrate her by comparison to the nurses at the office. We worked on her tirades and her outrageous behavior that alienated him, his office staff, and his family, and that left her feeling contemptible. Their sex life had improved because he was less demanding and she was less likely to balk and cause a fight. Their tenacious defensive system in which she was assigned the blame and was the repository for the rage, greed, ambition, and badness in the couple had not yet yielded to interpretation, although Rhonda was no longer on such a short fuse. I could see improvement in the diminution in the volume and frequency of her reactions and in the degree of his contempt, but the basic pattern stayed in place until Arthur felt safe enough to tell Rhonda and me the full extent of his sadistic and murderous fantasies in which he raped and axed various women who had abandoned him. Catharsis played a part in securing some relief for him, but the major therapeutic effect came from work done in the countertransference on the way he was treating the two actual women in the room with him, his wife and me, as he told his fantasies about other women.

As he concluded, Arthur said that he was terrified that people would think that he would act out his fantasies, which he had never done and would not do. Turning to me, he said, "You would understand that fear."

I felt extremely uncomfortable. If I acknowledged that I was familiar with such a fear, I felt I would be siding with him in assuming that his wife was ignorant.

Excluded and put down, Rhonda retorted, "You said *she* would understand, as if *I* wouldn't."

"She's a psychiatrist. She's heard all this before. She'll know I don't have any urges to do this in real sex," he replied.

Rhonda had a good point to make: "How does she know you're not gonna act those out? How do I know? Do *you* know? Because you seem really scared."

I said, "There is no evidence that Arthur will act out the fantasies in their murderous form. But there is evidence that he's scared they'll get out of hand. We also have evidence right here that you do sadistic things to each other in this relationship, not physically, but emotionally. 'Put-downs,' you call them."

"Like what just happened here!" exclaimed Rhonda. "Sure, she's trained, but I can understand it, too."

"Not that I'm gonna go out and do it," he reminded her.

"Right," she rejoined. "It's how you're gonna feel it. Arthur, I feel so relieved that it's not just been me. All these years I've been taking the shit for fucking up the marriage. Do you know, I feel so relieved. Finally, after all these years he's taking responsibility. Finally."

"But I told you about my sadistic fantasies," he said.

"You never did," Rhonda objected. "I'm not saying you never talked about fantasies before, but you never went into your real self, never in this detail. You've always said that I'm this, I'm that. It's always been me. Now I see in our marriage that your fantasies are totally in the way. Now *rape* I could maybe see as exciting, but why do you have to picture *murders*? That is scary."

I said, "To some extent the threatening part of the fantasy is arousing to both of you. But by the end of it, Arthur, you are terrified of losing control, and Rhonda, you are frightened for your life." They were nodding thoughtfully. I went on, "We're not talking put down, here. We're talking put *out*. These are compelling and forceful fantasies."

"This has been a big interference to you and to us," Rhonda replied. "This is like what you would call a breakthrough for us."

I felt inclined to agree with Rhonda's evaluation. The longer Arthur kept the fantasy to himself, the more it seemed to be the real him, terrified of being found out, hidden inside yet demanding to be heard. Furthermore, the way it got heard was through projection into Rhonda, who identified with it:

in her rages and attacks on Arthur she gave expression to that attacking, chopping-up part of him, for which she had a valency. Meanwhile, he contained for her the greater calamity of the wish for death, a wish and fear that stemmed from early loss of an envied and hated older brother.

Working through the interpersonal expression of fantasies late in the mid-phase

Following the revelation, the Clarks had a session in which Rhonda talked of her continued sense of gratitude that her husband had shared his fantasies with her. Although she felt unusually tentative about responding to him sexually, she felt close to him and committed to working things out. For the first time, she felt an equal level of commitment from him. Summer was approaching and she was taking the children to visit her family in Maine for a month, as usual. Until now, Rhonda had viewed her annual summer trip as a chance to get away from Arthur's criticizing her and demanding sex of her. For the first time, she felt sad that they would have to spend the summer apart.

The sharing of the fantasy had been a healing experience. The couple could now move beyond a level of functioning characteristic of the paranoid-schizoid position toward the depressive position in which there is concern for the object whose loss can be appreciated.

In a session following their vacation, Rhonda reported that she had gotten so much from the last session that it kept her thinking and working for four weeks. Even when Arthur expressed no affection during his phone call to her in Maine, when he did not even say he missed her, she felt hurt but not outraged as before. She realized that in some way he just wasn't there.

I suggested that Arthur had been unaware of feeling angry that Rhonda had left him alone for a few weeks and had dealt with it by killing her off.

"I was kind of pissed off at her being in Maine, getting to lie around on the family boat," Arthur admitted.

"He just cut me dead," Rhonda confirmed.

I said, "Well, there's the fantasy of killing operating again."

"Right," Rhonda replied. "But I didn't take it personally. It's just him. These last two weeks, I've been able to have grown-up feelings. Even though he belittles me, I don't live in a world of little feelings any more. That's a big change for me."

Arthur's revelation of his murderous fantasies released Rhonda's capacity for growth and informed both of them that the silent operation of the unconscious projective identification expressed in the fantasy had been cutting her down and killing off her adult capacities.

The individual's use of cultural fantasy

We are not limited to using unconscious fantasies that are the product of the patient's imagination alone. We also work with cultural fantasies, such as the themes of movies or books referred to by the patient. The associations of the patient (or of the family) are used to understand the meaning of this conscious fantasy that connects to unconscious fantasies. The personal emphasis or distortion of elements of a story or movie whose plot is known provides information about the patient's internal object relations and the way in which those operate. For instance, in response to the movie *The Prince of Tides,* in which a woman psychiatrist encourages her patient's brother to remember and reveal repressed and suppressed family history, in the course of which she falls in love with him, four patients responded quite differently and idiosyncratically. One patient was most affected by the trauma of the man's remembered rape scene and through it recovered her own anguish over being raped years before. The second patient to mention the movie focused on the healing aspect of the affair between the man and the psychiatrist in order to repress her retaliatory aggression against her promiscuous husband. The third patient, a woman who was unconsciously defending against homoerotic feelings for her female therapist, was most upset by the psychiatrist's enactment of her erotic countertransference. The fourth patient, a man who had resented his mother's seductive attachment to his brother, focused on the psychiatrist's denial that her lover, who was her patient's brother, was really in treatment with her, too, and therefore should have been protected from his wish to seduce her by her adherence to a clear code of ethics.

Working with fantasy expressed in play

Children may share their fantasies verbally but more commonly express them in the form of play. Through play, the child can speak for issues that the grown-ups may be more defended against.

The Warrens (more fully described as the W. family in *Foundations of Object Relations Family Therapy,* Chapter 24) consulted us for help in managing the clinging behavior of their toddler. In a diagnostic session, Mr. and Mrs. Warren talked with us while their daughters Terri, age 4, and Brooke, age 16 months, played beside them. The children's play expressed fantasies about separation from the preoedipal mother and inclusion or exclusion from the primal scene of the parents in intercourse.

Mr. Warren complained that his wife did not keep the house immaculate. She felt overwhelmed by his expectations and by having to run the household and manage two young children without help. She spoke of missing her mother, who lived far away and whom she used to call on for support and advice. As she spoke, Brooke sat on her mother's lap, sucking her pacifier, a visual image of her mother's longing.

Typical of a 4-year-old, Terri made a low, enclosed building on the floor with animals in and around it. Two sheep were inside and Oscar the Grouch was coming outside.

The play spoke to us of a fantasy of leaving the mother–child dyad. The one who left might be grouchy. But did the sheep couple represent the mother–infant couple from whom Terri was excluded, or that Brooke must now separate from, or the parental couple from whose bedroom both girls were excluded?

As the parents spoke more heatedly about their differences, Brooke left her mother's lap and messed up Terri's game. Terri punched her and Brooke returned to her mother's lap. The parents had to interrupt their discussion to deal with the fight.

David suggested that the girls had fought to divert the parents from their fight. But Mrs. Warren corrected him, saying that the girls interrupted *any* time that the parents talked together. Mrs. Warren went on to describe Terri's insistence on being heard and on interrupting her parents' conversations.

"So, Terri wants to bust up Mother's and Father's being together, as well as Mother and Brooke's closeness," I (JSS) said.

Terri and Brooke responded to this interpretation in play. Both girls now played without conflict. Terri had Oscar the Grouch peek out at some cows who he hoped might want to play with him. "He's wondering what they are doing," she explained. Terri's play suggested to us her feeling of exclusion from the parents' excitement, her hope of inclusion, her oedipal curiosity, and her desire to watch them. Brooke put dolls in cars and said Bye-Bye to them. Brooke's play indicated that she was getting on with her task of practicing separation. Each girl had responded to anxiety about the parents' relationship in ways colored by their age-appropriate concerns.

Terri continued to play with the animals and said that the horse outside the barn was lonely, but the two sheep were not because they had each other. Mrs. Warren spoke feelingly of her attachment to her mother, with whom she would go out shopping every weekend, leaving her father at home to make a perfect job of his home and garden. Later, Brooke got in the doll bed herself and lay still as a corpse. Then Mrs. Warren told of how her father had died one weekend in his garden when she was 19 years old.

We had been led by the children's play to understand the unconscious fantasy that when two people are close, it will cause the death of a third. Oedipal concerns about rivalry and exclusion could not be solved because of worries about killing. In fantasy, loss of the third party pushed the person back to the earlier dyad for safety. When Mrs. Warren felt this way, it was hard for her to let her child separate, and it was troubling to be close to her husband over her children's objections. It was also hard for her to keep a neat house, because her father's compulsion to do so was seen as having killed him.

Children reveal their unconscious fantasies in their play, much as adults do in reporting fantasies or dreams. In couple and family therapy, the individual shares his fantasy verbally or through play and the family cooperates to associate to it. What we find is that a fantasy may have been unconscious until now but, nevertheless, has found expression in symptomatology and has gained living form in the nature of the relationships within the family. In object relations therapy, we aim to make unconscious fantasy conscious in order to interrupt its destructive effect on family relationships now and to modify the internalization of internal objects based upon them.

NOTES

Dreams, conscious and unconscious fantasies, and children's play all offer a route to the unconscious:

Dreams (Freud 1900).
Endopsychic structure revealed in dreams (Fairbairn 1944).
Use of fantasy in couple therapy (D. Scharff and J. Scharff 1991).
Use of play in family therapy (J. Scharff 1989a, D. Scharff and J. Scharff 1987).

THIRTEEN

Technique and Theory Review with Clinical Illustration Focusing on the Use of Countertransference in Object Relations Family Therapy

CAN YOU REVIEW THE PRINCIPLES OF THEORY AND TECHNIQUE THROUGH A CLINICAL EXAMPLE FROM FAMILY THERAPY, FOCUSING ESPECIALLY ON COUNTERTRANSFERENCE AND INTERPRETATION?

(This clinical example is drawn from a case presented in Chapters 4, 10, and 12 of *Object Relations Family Therapy*. Here, David describes the case and his countertransference. We comment on his experience and relate it to concepts.)

130

My (DES) countertransference to the Jansens was well seasoned, after seeing them for almost two years. Mr. and Mrs. Jansen originally came to see me because Tom, then 9 years old, had broken into an electrical store and destroyed a lot of equipment. They explained that although he was a good kid basically, he was regularly the butt of teasing at school. Incidentally, they added, what really got to them most was the endless fighting with his two older brothers — Tom bullied them, even though he was two years younger.

Right away, I was struck with the denial in their presentation. Like many parents, they wanted it both ways. In their fantasy, they had a boy who was a good kid; nothing was wrong really. But in reality, they had a troubled boy who needed help. They wanted me to fix him without making them face his need to be fixed.

While I evaluated the situation, I absorbed the difficulty. Part of it lay between the parents. Mr. Jansen was the more controlling parent. His wife had been in psychotherapy for some time and had faced the family difficulty rather openly, but Mr. Jansen alternated between being proud of Tom's aggressiveness and close to despair. His brittleness left me feeling that it would be easy to say the wrong thing to this man, who I quickly came to feel could be so hurt that he would withdraw from the scene.

The couple's own differences added up to a marital problem, but they told me little about it. Mrs. Jansen told me in an individual session that they had sexual problems and that they fought often, much of it about Tom, sometimes over the other boys. But she was quick to confirm that her husband was thin-skinned about this, and she felt they would not be able to deal with the marital conflict, at least not for a while.

So I was left, right in the beginning, with a substantial countertransference to the parents' restrictions which kept me from operating the way I wanted to and from saying the things I felt should be said.

Monitoring therapist responses

The feelings that David developed in response to the encounter with this family are the ordinary lot of therapists. While the growth of these feelings could be understood as a reasonable and unremarkable response to dealing with difficult or controlling people, our experience has taught us that it is more usefully regarded as a noteworthy series of markers to be used in charting therapists' paths while orienting themselves and beginning the process of taking in families' difficulties. It is through this emotional charting of such encounters that we absorb the families' inner experience.

I understood the family's difficulty with trust and the controlling behavior of Mr. Jansen to represent a shared family difficulty: they had not been able to offer Tom all that he needed to steer a satisfactory course, and they were afraid that I would not be able to, either. Mr. Jansen had an expectation or transference that anyone in authority was likely to harm him and the family, and this was his way of trying to manage that possibility. But he was not alone in this feeling. When Mrs. Jansen expressed a more open position, she did so without conviction and with a fear of her own that if I pursued things too directly with her husband, he would rebel and refuse to get Tom and the family the help she thought they needed. In sum, they shared a feeling that outsiders could do them harm and that there was considerable question as to whether they could be helpful. And they tenderly guarded their own fears that something was wrong, lest they expose their fear that they had caused harm to someone they loved.

In getting this message across to me, in filling me with their own doubts and leaving me hamstrung, they had imparted more to me than a warning. They had shared the anxious worries so that I became like them in a way: full of feeling that the world of working with them was a tentative place, that it was hard to know where to walk without stepping on a landmine. And I felt I began to know what life was like for them, from the inside.

Gathering responses in the countertransference

The case of the Jansen family shows how countertransference can be a vehicle for understanding a family in depth through temporarily sharing their reality. During engagement with families, parts of therapists' own internal worlds are stirred in an internal resonance that illuminates for the therapists the meaning of the family's struggles. The process starts from the beginning, from the way a family enters the therapist's office. This interplay is part of every session. Our way of working with families is built on the experience that if we are willing to join families by making sense of our internal encounter with them, we will then be able to understand families in depth. We can then offer a level of understanding that has the power to transform the families and the relationships of family members to each other.

In the initial family session, Tom erupted at his two brothers and then ran out of the room to the car. Mr. and Mrs. Jansen were unable to persuade him to return. When I met with the parents the following week, Mr. Jansen would not allow Tom's brothers to be seen in family therapy. He said, "One of our sons has gone to the dogs; we aren't going to let him contaminate the ones who are okay."

Tom was not the only balky member of the family. Mr. Jansen would not agree to participate in family meetings either. He agreed readily to individual therapy for Tom, and he agreed to come for monthly parent guidance meetings with his wife as long as we focused on Tom. Mr. Jansen said, "I want you to understand that this is not to be therapy for us!"

It was the only contract the parents would allow, so I accepted it, with the hope that things would go well enough for them to trust me more over time, and we might eventually expand the work to include family therapy and perhaps couple therapy. After about six months, Tom's behavior improved enough at home and at school. A "trial family session" went without severe disruption, and Mr. Jansen agreed to expose all the children to family therapy.

My countertransference had by now become weathered by the work with this family. I was used to the couple's dance of vulnerability in which their shared fear was that I would harm one or the other by discrediting their parenting. I had become more sensitive to the fear of being victimized that they shared—a fear lived out in Tom's being picked on at school. When I felt bullied by them in the sessions, I had come to know that we were not far from their own fears that I would bully them, a derivative of the fear that each member of the family would turn bully to the others.

And things had gotten better. Tom was no longer the scapegoat for marital difficulties. We had been able to discuss his penchant for picking up the strain in his parents' marriage and in the family and his self-destructive attempts to solve their problems by making himself an object of concern by his delinquent behavior. We had discovered that at the point he had broken into the electrical shop, his mother had been threatened with a serious illness and the marriage had been in crisis. The family had learned a great deal about taking back their projective and introjective identifications.

Demonstrating projective and introjective identification and internal object relations

The term *projective identification* was coined by Klein to denote the unconscious process of projecting parts of the self outside the self and into others, dealing with the others as though they were then characterized by those parts of the self. The parts that are projected out may be hated parts of the self or object — let's say, a sense of badness or weakness — or they may be treasured parts that feel too endangered to survive inside the self. *Introjective identification* is the complementary process, in which a person takes in the projections of the other to solve an internal problem and then acts in identification with those parts.

Klein's concepts of projective and introjective identification are even more useful when put together with Fairbairn's theory of object relations. He held that it is the fundamental human need for a relationship that motivates psychological growth and development throughout life. He suggested that infants and children organize their psychological structure by taking in experience with their mothers and fathers, in the form of *internal objects,* which then form the basic building blocks of psychic structure.

The term *internal object* is really a technical one. It does not imply that personal relationships are to be understood in mechanized ways. Rather, the word *object* stems from Freud's use in which one person was described as the "object" of the sexual and aggressive drives of the other. Freud did not use the term *internal object*, but he did describe introjection of the object of the drives in states of loss of the object. For some people, a better term than *internal object relations* might well be *internalized personal relations,* but the use of the word *object* has persisted because it continues an important tradition of clinical theory begun by Freud, Klein, and Fairbairn.

These internal objects are closely related to parts of the self, and the relationship between a part of the self and an internal object forms the structure of an internal object *relationship.* In projective identification, the intolerably painful parts of these internal, unconscious relationships are split off and put outside the self and into another person. For the process to be complete, the other person must be partly taken over by them without quite knowing it. That is, there must also be a complementary introjective identification in another person for the transactional part of projective identification to be complete. In this way, projective and introjective identification become the vehicles for unconscious communication. In all intimate relationships, projective identification is a mutual process that is the normal basis for unconscious understanding and empathy. When it is skewed, it is also the basis for shared unconscious misunderstanding and for unconsciously collusive pathology.

Mr. Jansen projected his unconscious sense of weakness onto

his wife and Tom. Mrs. Jansen projected strength and even stubbornness into her husband, and went along with that part of herself that she found in him. And Tom projected his inner goodness and strength into others, taking in through introjective identification the sense of weakness and badness for the family, unconsciously hoping to leave the rest of his family better off in the process.

I had accumulated this sense of them and their improvement, when the three of them entered my office about a year after the beginning of the weekly family sessions. The two older boys had been attending regularly. There was usually a lot of brotherly bickering. The work had enlarged the three boys' awareness of many of the family issues. After the previous session, the two older boys had left for a month at camp. In this report, I will detail my own responses in order to illustrate the progress and use of countertransference during a single session.

Tom sat in a red swivel chair, in which he rotated during much of the session, to Mr. Jansen's annoyance. Mrs. Jansen said they had not fought this week in any way, unlike last week, when they had fought on the way to the session. Tom had used this in the session against his father. Mr. Jansen said that all of them, even Tom, were missing the older boys.

"Sure I am," said Tom. "They're my brothers."

"But you used to fight so much!" said Mrs. Jansen.

"Well, we love each other. That's just the way brothers are," said Tom. "But I also like having the house to myself."

So far, I felt this was an interesting byplay, and I noted that Tom did indeed seem fonder of his absent brothers than he would have admitted to being a year earlier. Already, I had a countertransference sense of uneasiness about the way the parents were getting him to show off his progress, but I appreciated it partly too, as if it were a credit to my helpfulness to them. I had the idea, "They're showing off as if giving a 'report card' on Tom's improvement."

My thought was confirmed a moment later, when Mr. Jansen said that they had gotten Tom's school report card. As he said this, Tom began to get silly and blow in the air, making noises, and turning in his chair. Both parents got angry at this, telling him to stop, but he did not stop for some time. This was the kind of thing that made them mad at home.

Finally, Mr. Jansen said, "Tom, no ice cream if you don't stop!"

"That's blackmail!" yelled Tom.

"Sure it is," said Father, "and I mean it!"

Tom now continued the behavior, while also beginning to pout. He was daring his father, who said again, "Tom! I mean it. No ice cream!"

Mr. Jansen said this in such a manner that I experienced a dance between them, in which Tom would give in just in time to get his ice cream. I felt both frustrated for Mr. Jansen that Tom would not stop, and annoyed with him for setting Tom up in the first place. I had confused and contradictory feelings about the "report" on school progress and on Tom's growth: it seemed to me that Mr. Jansen had gotten away with showing off Tom's increased ability to express love for his brothers. Why did he have to rub it in about school? And I thought that there must be some embarrassment on Tom's part about doing well at school.

Though I could not quite formulate it in the hour, afterward I realized that Mr. Jansen was doing just the kind of showing off and flaunting that probably got Tom in trouble at school. Tom was doing the clowning, which probably accompanied his own wish to show off his "brilliance." Since he had been improving, he now knew better than to do it, but he was being provoked by his father.

At this point in the hour, I was feeling unsure of what was happening, and vaguely uncomfortable both with Mr. Jansen and with Tom. My discomfort was partly with Tom's clowning which did not seem to be due to his discomfort. All

I could feel was that he was showing off. And I was uncomfortable with Mr. Jansen's persistent use of threats, which felt to me to be retaliatory and empty instead of constituting effective limit setting. I now recalled that I had been feeling annoyed with Mr. Jansen for the times he had urged Tom to slug kids when they teased him. I would start out feeling sure that was not a good solution, but Mr. Jansen and Tom managed to present these situations in which Tom was picked on in such a way that I could no longer quite tell what I thought. I knew that my own history of peer relations in latency and early adolescence made this an area in which I am a bit vulnerable, which means that I have to think through a solution each time, rather than relying on innate sense, as I might in other areas. So I had ended up slightly confused and thinking, "Well, perhaps it is the thing to do after all."

Using negative capability

Here is a potentially valuable opportunity for the therapist. David finds the family in a moment of affective intensity and at the same time experiences in himself some confusion. This indicates that he is in touch with object relationships that are active in the session. Not that it is uncommon for a therapist to be uncertain, or to need to wait for a while to know where things will settle out, but this confusion was different: it represented David's losing his way inside himself. Moments like these are especially valuable, and we urge beginning therapists to tolerate them. This capacity to "not know" is captured in the term *negative capability* borrowed from the poet Keats. In one of his letters, Keats described Shakespeare's poetic quality of allowing meaning to emerge from inside an experience, rather than needing to impose ideas on experience with unreasonable speed, before the richness of an experience has blossomed. This tolerance of "not knowing" and of confusion allows meaning to emerge from within the therapist, and adds a dimension of richness to the encounter that can only be achieved by new discovery from the inside. This type of countertransference experience sheds light on a core affective experience in the therapy session and leads to a deeper level of understanding.

In the hour, I only knew that my discomfort was a time-tested sign that there was also conflict and confusion in the patients and that this was the time to intervene by exploring their confusion. I noticed that Mrs. Jansen was sitting by and letting this go on, as she often did. At that moment, I thought of her as leaving things to Mr. Jansen, but slightly smirking as she did so.

As I thought of these things, Mr. Jansen was going on to tell about the achievement in the report card which was excellent after Tom's shaky start at the beginning of the year.

As the tension eased, I felt ready to use my therapeutic discomfort to advantage before the moment passed.

I interrupted Mr. Jansen, hoping to help the family stay with the themes of blackmailing and difficult behavior. I wanted to enlarge their capacity for observation and to help them include an understanding of the history of old experience that led up to this moment. I began with a question that might link the events in the therapy hour with Tom's difficulties elsewhere. I said, "Is this exchange in here between Dad and Tom anything like Tom's being picked on at school—which Tom really doesn't like Dad or Mom to discuss, but which together you may be re-creating in the session?"

Mr. Jansen was thrown off stride by my question, because it interrupted him as he was charging ahead over Tom's objection. I could see by the way I had confused him in the process that my own discomfort had led me to intervene less smoothly than I would have wished. Mr. Jansen, however, was not too thrown off to respond, so we got by this moment.

He said, "I 'blackmail' him because I don't know what else to do. How do you stop him?" he asked. "But I can see that it might relate to school." He paused, looking down.

Then he looked at Tom again and said, "Tom, did you know that I used to get in a lot of fights when I was a kid? And I used to lose!" And as he said this, Mr. Jansen's tone relaxed and he seemed to change from being in a head-on collision with Tom to being in a loving, fatherly position.

I could hardly believe the tone of Mr. Jansen's sharing. It was spontaneous and earnest, a new way of presenting himself. I felt relief and a pang of hope that this new opening might signal a breakthrough.

Tom said just, "No! I didn't know that. Did you?" He then stopped playing with the cards he had been fiddling with after he gave up swivelling the chair, and he looked straight at his father.

My feeling for Mr. Jansen was shifting. This was a moment in which I realized, again more in retrospect than I could consciously get a grip on in the hour, how much I had felt bullied by Mr. Jansen right from the beginning when he took such an outrageous stance about the "contamination of his good sons" and had used that as a front to avoid investigating or sharing his part in Tom's troubles. Although I felt sympathetic on one level with Mrs. Jansen's tolerance of his bullying, my going along with her in not pressuring him to contribute had meant that I had felt vicariously bullied, too. But this episode, with its small evidence of willingness to share, suddenly let me feel that I liked Mr. Jansen more than before. And since I knew how hard it was for him to let down his guard, I felt respect for him with his newfound courage.

Object relations history at moments of affective exchange

One of the basic techniques of object relations family therapy is to ask the family at moments of intense exchange of feelings to share old experiences that seem to be like the current problem or impasse. These moments of core affective exchange offer more than history. They actually describe the way old relationships determine current history because they are carried alive inside the individual family members. These old internal object relationships exist inside all individual family members and have a great influence on current relationships. David intended to ask Mr. Jansen about such an old experience in the next few moments, but Mr. Jansen beat him to the punch—a good sign that family and therapist were working well together.

Led by my internal experience, I asked Mr. Jansen to say more. This time he elaborated, slightly sheepishly, but willingly:

"I was athletic, which helped. But the older kids would come by and it would always be me they picked on. I couldn't beat them up. It wasn't quite like with Tom. It wasn't the kids my own age who did it, but I did get beat up—often!"

I was thinking, slightly angrily still, that I understood something about how he got them to do this so regularly, that is, I was assuming he must have been provocative. As he made the brief statement about the older boys picking on him, I had a brief scene pass through my head in which I saw him taunting some older boys and saw them ganging up on him. In having this fantasy, I was identified partly with him and partly with the older boys, and partly I saw it from the perspective of my childhood self. I had some sympathy for him, and some for his attackers.

As I was pondering this, Mrs. Jansen said, "I wonder if you didn't do something to provoke them?"

I followed her by saying I had been thinking that Mr. Jansen often seemed to be wanting Tom to fight as a solution to being teased. Since we had been thinking together about how Tom might be provoking the other kids, I wondered if this might fit with his encouraging Tom to cause trouble, even though he was worried about it.

Mrs. Jansen smiled and said, "Oh, my husband can be provocative himself, you know. He does it with me, for a start."

Mutual projective identification in the marriage

This moment in the hour began another important direction, critical to the therapeutic task. Mrs. Jansen had taken the lead in linking the total situation, and the work so far in the hour, to their marriage. It is important to understand links between the projective identifications, like the one Mr. Jansen had to Tom, but most especially to any similar dynamic in the marriage.

In an object relations approach to the family, the dynamics of the family at large are understood to be built on the foundation of the marital relationship. The mutual projective identifications between the parents set the tone for the overall pattern of the family. When a link can be made in therapy between a parent--child object relationship and the parents' relationship, the family's understanding is greatly enhanced. At this point, the family was not only willing to attempt this work, but was initiating it — a sign of therapeutic progress. The more therapeutic the family can be for itself and the greater the working alliance between therapist and family, the sooner the family will be ready for termination.

"Can you give me an example of how he is provocative with you?" I asked.

Mrs. Jansen thought for a moment and said, "There was the time you were supposed to pick me up and we got our signals crossed."

Mr. Jansen filled in the story: his wife had come home in a blue fury after having to walk a good deal of the way home because she had no money with her. He knew she was mad when she walked in the door.

"Yes," she said, "but instead of even saying you were sorry I had to walk, you accused me of stupidity in not knowing which corner was which, and you said it served me right. I admit that I was too mad to begin with, but that's not the point right now. You used it to provoke me." And she smiled, quite fondly, to let him know she was not attacking him, and finished, "And you know it, honey!"

"It's true," he said. "I do that to her, and I kind of enjoy it. I shouldn't, but it's true that I do."

I noted that they had managed this piece of the work themselves. I noticed a kind of "hats off to them" feeling. I realized that I was feeling proud of them for holding together to do this work.

Having gotten the fact of provocation within the family onto the table, I felt we could try to link it to Tom. So I turned to him and asked if he knew about this part of his father's life.

"Well, I know he can tease Mommy and me," he said. "But, I never knew about the fights with the older kids. That's pretty interesting, Dad!"

I now felt emotionally included in a family whose members were not bullying each other and provocatively keeping me outside the group. I felt we were working together in a new way, so that I could try to make a new kind of interpretation that might not, at this moment, meet the usual family unconscious resistance.

I said, "I wonder, Mr. Jansen, if you think you might want Tom to pick off a few of the tormentors for you, a sort of vicarious victory over the kids who used to beat on you?"

"I never thought of that," he said. "Perhaps so."

Because of my understanding and surviving his bullying, and because of his wife's loving confrontation and support, Mr. Jansen was able to accept this interpretation. Mrs. Jansen now put her arm around his shoulder. I thought that because of the gains in this session, in the future we might be able to talk about the way people felt picked on in the family as the original version of Tom's being picked on by his peers at school.

So I said, "The two issues—feeling picked on at home and at school—are related." Speaking with conviction gained from understanding my own feeling of being bullied in this therapeutic session, I added, "Understanding feeling picked on at home ought to help figure out what happens at school."

Tom was interested! At the door he said an unusually cheerful good-bye!

WHAT IS THE ROLE OF INTERPRETATION?

Interpretation, whether spoken by the therapist or by a family member, is a building block in the joint construction of increased understanding. It is not a pronouncement from above, but a shared matter, to be tested, modified, and slowly accepted or discarded in favor of other ways of understanding. In this sense, interpretation is not an end product or something to be valued in itself, but a catalyst for developing shared understanding. In object relations theory, understanding is thought to be crucial in the development of the individual. Mother and baby, lovers, spouses, and family devote themselves to understanding each other's needs. A relationship is not only a matter of getting along or surviving together, but of providing for emotional growth through mutual understanding. Similarly, in object relations therapy we promote understanding.

HOW IS COUNTERTRANSFERENCE USED?

In object relations therapy, countertransference is used to enhance and guide therapists' understanding and to inform their interventions. The therapist works by joining with the individual patient's, couple's, or family's experience and allowing it to get inside, and then working together until the experience is understood. Shared understanding is the vehicle for that sense of joining. Counter-transference represents the therapist's sharing of the experience, one that is in resonance with the internal life of the therapist. When therapists have been able to make sense of the countertrans- ference, they let the patient, couple, or family know of their understanding by giving them feedback. At the simplest level, this feedback consists of making links or clarifying what the therapists have understood. At the highest level, feedback is given in the form of interpretation, based in the countertransference. Coun-tertransference is the material of the therapist's work. It is the guide that the therapist uses to join the individual or family in restoring them to emotional flexibility and growth. Along the way, it offers the therapist many opportunities for growth as well.

NOTES

Clinical vignettes from long-term combined individual, child, and family therapy illustrate and review concepts that we have already presented. As in therapy, so in teaching we cover the same patterns in slightly different ground:

Projective and introjective identification, object relations (Klein 1946).
Introjection of the object (Freud 1921).
Internal object relationship, object relations and object relations theory (Fairbairn 1952, 1963).
Keats's term "negative capability" (Murray 1955).
Core affective exchange (Scharff and Scharff 1987).
Mutual projective identification in marriage (Zinner 1976).
Interpretation (Strachey 1934, Stewart 1990).
Countertransference (Freud 1910a, Racker 1968, Scharff and Scharff 1987, 1991, D. Scharff 1992, J. Scharff 1992).

FOURTEEN

Working Through
and Termination

HOW DOES WORKING THROUGH
TAKE PLACE?

Working through was Freud's term for continued analysis of resistance that persisted and intensified as layers of repression were peeled away. In object relations terms we think of working through as a clarification and resolution of projective identificatory patterns. Projective identifications have to be experienced over and over at progressively higher levels of development. Sometimes when the pattern recurs, we may have an inevitable "here-we-go-again" feeling. Sometimes we may feel hopeless that the patient will ever maintain gains and get better. We note, however, that the periods in which the patient is operating at the paranoid-schizoid end of the continuum are shorter. Patients can recognize their projective identifications through which they relate to the therapist. Applying the understanding and containing function internalized from experience with their mature therapists, patients can metabolize and detoxify their projective identifications for themselves. Sometimes the work of this phase seems boring, especially to the therapist who enjoys discovery and catharsis. But the laborious work of standing by while the patient learns the maintenance of good self-functioning is essential. Our boredom is a defense against recognizing that we are about to become redundant. We must take our pleasure, like a good parent, from recognizing the patient's progress, independence, and autonomy.

WHAT ABOUT TERMINATION?

The individual, couple, or family is ready to terminate when they have returned to the appropriate developmental phase of individual or family life from which level any regression is temporary and can be resolved by self-analytic functioning. Readiness for termination can be recognized from improvement in the capacities outlined in Table 14–1:

Table 14–1. Signs of Readiness for Termination
Improved capacity
1. to master developmental stress
2. to work cooperatively
3. to have loving object relationships
4. to integrate hate with love and tolerate ambivalence
5. to perceive others accurately
6. to have empathy and concern for others
7. to differentiate among and meet the needs of the individual

We aim for these wide goals. We are not interested in terminating as soon as symptom resolution is achieved. The termination will occur when the criteria for termination have been met. Specifically, and in the technical sense, we look for signs that the following criteria for termination shown in Table 14–2 have been met:

Table 14–2. Criteria for Termination
1. The therapeutic space has been internalized and a reasonably secure holding capacity has been formed.
2. Unconscious projective identifications have been recognized, owned, and taken back.
3. The capacity to work together with family members or life partners is restored.
4. Intimate and sexual relating is now gratifying and satisfying.
5. The individual can provide good holding for the self, and the couple or family can provide a vital holding environment for the individual, couple, or family.
6. The capacity to mourn the loss of the therapeutic relationship is sufficient to support a satisfactory termination and to prepare the patient, couple, or family to deal with future developmental losses and to envision their future beyond therapy.

CAN YOU SHOW AN EXAMPLE FROM INDIVIDUAL THERAPY OF READINESS FOR TERMINATION AFTER WORKING THROUGH?

Mrs. Epstein (mentioned in Chapter 10) had been in a prolonged working-through phase in her analysis with me (JSS). She had worked on her projective identification of me, in which I was all that was wonderful and she was nothing. She had discovered how her envy of me (and originally of her mother and her mother's exciting relationship to her husband) had depleted her self-worth. Her fantasy solution had been that if only she could stay with me forever, or get from me what I had, or become me, she could feel good about herself. We went over this fantasy again many times in many different forms until she became able to relate to me as an equal in a collaborative relationship. Previously unable to enjoy what she had, she could now enter her life and give and receive love fully. Formerly unemployable, she could now earn a good salary. It was clear that she was close to termination.

But Mrs. Epstein had lost her mother by sudden death in a car crash when she was just 12 years old, shortly after her first menstrual period. She got the idea that growth and autonomy killed the person she had depended on. Separation meant death to her, and so termination was to be feared and would require a final piece of working through. After a dreadful experience of deadness and emptiness during her last summer break — which stood for her final separation from analysis — Mrs. Epstein became terrified of terminating in case that would be how she would feel afterward. She saw that this was her fantasy, based on her earlier loss, and that, unlike that time, she and I could go on living separately after termination. A wonderful dream reassured her of her capacity to have a good good-bye, and she recovered her previous level of functioning within two weeks.

There were some short-lived regressions, but in general, Mrs. Epstein continued to be independent, assertive, competitive, and compassionate toward me. She talked of a feeling of new energy, space, and confidence, with plenty of love to give. She talked of having the good times and the bad times balanced clearly in her mind. She said that she thought that she had retrieved past experience, mended it, and fused past and present into something that would serve the future. She was not worried when I missed a day because of sickness, and she did not get mad at being reminded when a patient came too early for his session that someone would be taking her place. Her capacity for self-analysis, for integration of experience, and for recovery from setbacks was consistently in evidence. Her experience of my therapeutic capacity was fully internalized. She no longer needed me and she could at last feel that she had something to give me. Mrs. Epstein was ready to terminate. As she left, she said, "Like the bulbs I've just had planted, what we've done together is in. It's real. I don't have to see it to know it's there. It's not just mine. It's yours, too. But the flowers will be mine."

Mrs. Epstein happened to go the distance in her analysis. Not all patients have such determination and fortitude, or such ambitious goals for their development. We want to be sure that we support patients' or clients' criteria for termination rather than imposing our own. Although we have our own views of what constitutes readiness for termination, we do not want our own therapeutic ambitions to define patients' goals.

NOTES

When repression is undone, further resistance against the emergence of conflict needs to be worked through. When conflict is sufficiently expressed, experienced, and understood in terms of patterns of unconscious communication, we can say that the working through is completed. This development ushers in the termination phase:

Working through (Freud 1914, Scharff and Scharff 1987).
Termination (Scharff and Scharff 1987)

III

Application and Integration

FIFTEEN

Integration of Individual Therapy with Couple, Family, Group, and Sex Therapies

HOW IS INTEGRATION OF DIFFERENT MODALITIES POSSIBLE?

Integration of individual therapy with couple, family, group, and sex therapies is easy because they share the same theoretical model in which the individual personality consists of a self that contains and relates to internal objects that represent the person's experience with the family of origin. Parts of the self or object are then projected into the significant others—spouse, therapist, family members—in a stuck cycle or in a new way that allows reworking. This happens in therapy, in long-term friendships, in marriage, in sexuality, and with each successive developmental stage.

Fairbairn gave us a view of the individual personality as a system of internal object relations in dynamic relation to each other. It was Dicks's genius to note that when two such personalities united in marriage, this formed a union in which each partner could project unwanted or endangered internal object relationships into the spouse, leading to a state of mutual projective identification. The partners sought to use the marriage to afford this opportunity for protection of the self of each spouse and their relationship. Unfortunately the mutual projective identification also often led to deterioration in the relationship between the spouses, who could not separately be whole persons because of their reliance on the combination of the two personalities to make them whole. The projective system between marital partners leads to a discernible marital joint personality.

Bion applied Kleinian theory to groups. He noted that projective identification occurs between the group and the leader, and among the individuals, to create an unacknowledged series of subgroups. These subgroups come together in order to express certain unconscious assumptions about what the group should be doing, feeling, and experiencing. Individuals get together according to these basic assumptions because of their individual valencies to do so. Similarly, we find that in marriage, spouses are chosen because of their valencies to accept particular projective identifications of their spouses. Shapiro and Zinner were the first to apply projective identification to families. They noted that adolescents were identified as harboring unwanted or longed-for parts of the parents and were then treated as symptomatic and pathological in an effort on the part of the family to isolate and at the same time take care of these disavowed parts. Shapiro and Zinner also described shared unconscious family assumptions, namely, unacknowledged but passively agreed-on views that organize the family and protect it from facing anxiety that it fears would disrupt or annihilate the family. Zinner applied this concept of mutual projective identification to the marital interaction of the parents in the families that he studied.

We have applied object relations theory to couple and family therapy and to sex therapy. The resulting object relations couple and family therapy is a method that derives from psychoanalytic principles shown in Table 15–1.

Table 15–1. Principles of Object Relations Therapy
1. Listening
2. Responding to unconscious material
3. Developing insight
4. Following affect
5. Working with dream and fantasy
6. Interpreting
7. Working in the transference and countertransference toward understanding and growth

The therapeutic relationship offers an environment similar enough for these patterns to emerge, but different enough for identification and reworking, because the therapist brings the capacity for holding, for sharing the couple's experience, for tolerating the anxiety involved, and for providing space for understanding.

CAN YOU SHOW AN EXAMPLE OF COMBINED, CONCURRENT, AND SERIAL FAMILY, INDIVIDUAL, AND SEX THERAPY?

Lars and Velia Simpson (described more fully in *Object Relations Couple Therapy,* Chapters 10 and 11) had been married since late adolescence. They loved each other and were committed to staying together, whether or not they could be helped. They were referred to me (DES) for consultation about their sexual difficulties. Velia, who had previously suffered from vaginismus and was still anorgasmic, had a total dislike of sex, and Lars had premature ejaculation. In a couple diagnostic session, I learned that Velia was from a family where the children looked to each other for affection — sometimes combined with sexual stimulation — in the absence of love and caring from their parents. Lars could remember little from his childhood, except that his parents got divorced after his father's arrest for homosexual solicitation when Lars was 17. His amnesia suggested earlier trauma. Lars and Velia were each other's first loves, the objects to which each escaped from unsatisfactory families.

In a single diagnostic family session, they reported that, when they fought over their frustration with their sex life, their children tended to get upset and cause diversionary trouble. As they alluded, without being inappropriately graphic, to what they called "difficulty with conjugal relations" the children did indeed start to fight. In general, their older son Eric tried to be good but seemed to catch his mother's rage anyway. Alex, their middle child, was hyperactive and so afraid to express anger that he was inclined to soil his pants. Jeanette, the youngest, was a cute and unabashedly seductive oedipal child who introduced sexual excitement into the family despite the grown-ups' fear of sex.

The parents agreed to my request for an extension of the consultation so that Alex could be evaluated individually. Psychometric testing showed that Alex had attention deficit disorder with hyperactivity. The parents accepted my recommendation of individual therapy for Alex with a psychiatrist who could combine psychotherapy with medication. Velia and Lars were not able to tolerate the idea of sex therapy, but they would have tried family therapy if a therapist could have been found for them. I could not take them on myself at that time, and there was no other family therapist at the clinic. During the consultation, Velia had recognized her underlying depression and accepted referral to a psychiatrist for three-times-a-week individual therapy for herself.

Individual therapy for Alex

It turned out that Alex was not motivated to be in therapy and could not benefit from it. His hyperactivity at school did benefit from stimulant medication, but his soiling, jealousy, and disruptiveness at home persisted and would require some other form of psychotherapy. I would discover that he was much more able to benefit from family therapy than he had from individual treatment. Our choice of modality is determined by the patient's demonstrated preference and capacity for working in a particular setting, as well as by the availability of therapists.

Individual therapy for Velia

Psychoanalytically oriented psychotherapy was combined with antidepressant medication and occasional brief hospitalization when Velia was suicidal. In the transference, she recovered a fantasy of herself as a sexy person who hid so as not to be seen as dirty by her therapist. She learned that she could feel sexual and express these feelings toward him without his responding to her longing with action. Assured of a safe environment, she found that her most repressed longing was for a trusted parent for whom she could feel longing without enactment of incestuous wishes.

Soon after Alex's individual therapy failed, and while Velia's individual therapy was ongoing, the Simpsons began family therapy with me, now that I had time to see them. In an early session, Velia talked with Lars and me about her fear of physical intimacy and her ensuing rage. The children's play reflected the theme and displayed the dynamics of the sexual difficulty in the context of the parents' relationship. Alex built a long tunnel out of blocks and called it a firehouse.

Jeanette drove a firetruck with an extension ladder through the firehouse and broke it apart. The parents recognized the children's play with the firetruck breaking the firehouse as a symbol of their fear of the destructive potential of intercourse. The children further contributed the idea that a girl who thinks that she should be the driver will always wreck things and that it would be better to have a boy driving the truck, quite a telling comment on the problem of Lars's trauma-based passivity. As the months went by, we continued to explore the family ramifications of the parents' sexual difficulty. We worked on understanding the parents' projective identifications of their children as aspects of their own abusive parents. But Velia and Lars were still too frightened to confront their sexual difficulties directly.

Sex therapy for Velia and Lars

Six months later, Lars and Velia began sex therapy with me in addition to weekly family therapy. In response to sex therapy assignments that restricted the fullness of their sexual expression, Velia experienced an enormous amount of agonized, irritable hyperexcitement, and Lars was afraid of the masturbation exercises. During the intense focus on physicality and forbidden sexual activity, Velia recovered memories of physical abuse by her father and sexual play with her adolescent brother, for whose penis she relived her longing and revulsion. Shortly thereafter, Lars, whose forgetting of his childhood was dense, recalled that his father had committed anal intercourse on him and that he, Lars, had then turned around and done the same to his brother. Each of them had a reason to feel intense shame about their longing for the penis. Having worked this through in relation to their histories and their embarrassing fantasies in their transferences to me, Lars and Velia became able to enjoy controlled sexual-arousal and intercourse together. A reversion to sexual failure occurred during my vacation, and this gave an opportunity to work on their response to me as an abandoning object. Unable to express their rage at me for being like their parents, who they felt did not care what happened to them, Lars and Velia could not bring their repressed rejecting object relationship to consciousness. It remained unconscious and expressed itself there by attacking their exciting object relationship. This internal way of dealing with rage at the object spoiled their capacity for sexual pleasure. In this way, they showed me rather than told me how I had hurt them. Rage was repressing longing. With further work, the Simpsons became able to tell me that they were mad at me and that they had missed me.

Before therapy, Lars and Velia suppressed their longing for closeness and gave vent to more rage than love. Bringing their sexuality to life through sex therapy and Velia's individual therapy threatened the couple with the revival of the bad fathers of their shared longing. In individual therapy, Velia reworked and owned her projective identifications in the transference. Sex therapy enabled Lars and Velia to express wishes to be loved and cared for in the shared transference to the sex therapist as an abandoning and later as a protective, nonincestuous, noninvasive object, after which they could transform each other into nontoxic sexual objects for each other to love and cherish. Family therapy relieved the children of the burden of provoking the parents' toxic projective identifications of them. The children's behavior changed so that they no longer inserted themselves in the war zone between their parents or created diversions from their parents' issues. With their intimate relationship repaired, Lars and Velia became more available as a parenting couple in whom their children could trust.

Because each form of therapy is built on the same basic theory, individual, couple, family, and sex therapy are theoretically and practically compatible with each other. The recommendation for an individual patient, couple, or family is based on a consideration of the fit of a suitable approach or of a mixture of modalities with the patient's preferences and readiness for therapy. Once we make an initial recommendation for a treatment plan, we want to try that treatment plan until we run into an impediment or further information that might cause us to reconsider it. For instance, we might recommend concurrent individual and family therapy and find that for some period of time this goes along well, with both therapies effective. Then, perhaps, the family work falls apart.

Imagine a session for a family of five where three members do not show up. This leaves the therapist with two "identified patients" who are there as if by accident at the convenience of the others. It is important not to change the therapeutic plan under this kind of pressure, but to use the experience to understand the family's resistance expressed in substituting individuals for a shared family group. The therapist hopes to reestablish the family commitment to therapy. If there is no response to interpretation of the resistance, and the two members continue to attend alone and to identify themselves as in need of help, the therapist might then agree to a change in the treatment format. Before offering to find another individual therapist for the second motivated family member, the therapist will work on acknowledging the loss of the motivated family and helping the remaining members to mourn the loss of the family treatment.

In other cases, movement from one format to another can be a sign of progress. When a family has improved its holding capacity in family therapy and is ready to terminate, the decision for one of its members to continue in individual therapy with the family's support is a sign of the family's newfound ability to differentiate among and meet the needs of its individual members. For instance, in a family where the mother had been sexually abused as a child, she did not have the confidence to tell her story outside the family. After family therapy was terminated, with her husband's unexpected encouragement, the woman was able to join a survivors-of-incest group. An individual may complete an analysis and later, facing unanticipated developmental challenge, may bring his family for family therapy. In the case described in Chapter 13, the parents refused family therapy. The 9-year-old boy was seen in individual therapy and the parents in parent guidance sessions. After developing trust in the therapist, the parents accepted the necessity for family meetings and the individual therapy continued. In *Object Relations Family Therapy* (Chapter 12), we described a case in which child analysis was combined productively with couple therapy for the parents. The important point is that switching from one format to another should not be a random response to resistance or transference enactment. Concurrent, combined, and serial therapy formats should be carefully and thoughtfully planned and then adhered to. As always, the frame of treatment is crucially important.

NOTES

Because object relations theory applies equally well to understanding individual, couple, and family dynamics, we find that individual, couple, family, and sex therapy methods can be compatible with one another when each is based in object relations theory. Combined, concurrent, or serial therapies can then be undertaken:

Fairbairn's view of internal object relations (Fairbairn 1963).
Mutual projective identification in marriage (Dicks 1967).
Basic assumption subgroups (Bion 1959).
Projective identification in families, shared unconscious family assumptions (Zinner and Shapiro 1972).
Mutual projective identification in marriage (Zinner 1989).
The integration of individual, couple, family, and sex therapy (Scharff and Scharff 1987, 1991).

SIXTEEN

The Application of Object Relations Theory to Various Syndromes and Populations

HOW DOES OBJECT RELATIONS THEORY APPLY TO ADDICTIONS COUNSELING?

For an autonomous symptom such as addiction to alcohol or drugs, a nondirective object relations therapy approach alone is not sufficient to deal with the problem. The person requires a supportive and rehabilitative network and a confrontational group system in which to be challenged with the need to stop the addictive habit, whose secondary effects make the psychodynamic treatment impossible in serious cases. However, giving up the addictive symptomatology is not the end of the treatment; but only the beginning of therapy. Object relations theory helps the addiction counselor to understand the problem that patient and counselor are facing.

Some patients at the higher end of development will be able to move rather promptly into a psychodynamic treatment and may not require the full course of detoxification, behavioral treatment, and group-based treatment. Those whose substance abuse is mild may give it up without group support and move directly into outpatient object relations therapy. This may happen in cases of substance abuse, but it is rarely successful in addiction.

We conceptualize the addictive substance as a representation of the exciting object for which the self longs and hungers. The symptom is a repetitive concretization of the introjective identification of the elusive nourishing object. In its absence, the self has lost the creative capacity to form symbols and find metaphors for describing and metabolizing experience. Instead, the self uses addictive, or in more severe cases, psychotic behaviors to communicate its pain to its external objects while attempting to obliterate its effects upon the self.

DOES OBJECT RELATIONS THERAPY HELP IN THE TREATMENT OF ANOREXIA NERVOSA?

Below a certain weight, management of the holding environment may have to include hospitalization to avoid death from starvation or heart attack due to fluid imbalance. Object relations theory helps us to conceptualize the patient's need to control food intake. Instead of eating as an automatic habit, the self uses food to enact its intrapsychic attitude to objects. As in addiction or alcoholism, there is a concretization of object relationships in terms of a substance, in this case food. Object relations therapy can be helpful in the transference work with such patients, who frequently hunger for and reject their therapist's intervention, much as they binge on food or chop it up into tiny pieces that do not add up to a full meal. Applied to the dysfunctional family system in which the anorexic patient has grown up, object relations theory illuminates the way that the starving person contains a family-wide anxiety about hunger and the female body. Before she turned her attention to the use of paradoxical interventions and universal prescriptions, Mara Selvini Palazzoli understood anorexia from an object relations perspective. Kent Ravenscroft has applied object relations family therapy in the treatment of bulimic adolescents.

IF CLIENTS NEED A PSYCHOEDUCATIONAL APPROACH, HOW CAN OBJECT RELATIONS THEORY BE HELPFUL?

This question is often asked concerning schizophrenic or chronically psychotic and disabled patients, mentally handicapped family members, and difficult-to-educate children, such as those with hyperactivity, severe learning and developmental difficulties, and severe behavioral problems.

When the capacity to learn is so impaired that psychological and cognitive growth and academic achievement cannot occur in the ordinary way, then the psychoeducational approach is the treatment of choice. The psychoeducational approach remediates the psychological interference with educational processes by (1) attuning the educational effort to the psychological needs and (2) treating the psychological disturbance so that the child or adult can make use of education and allow learning to occur. We think that object relations therapy is applicable to treating the psychological disturbance, but its use has been debated by some experts in the treatment of the learning-disabled, neurobiologically impaired, and psychotic populations. Committed to the view that the symptom resides in the index patient, these experts object to methods that explore the object relations history or the family dynamics because they think that such an approach blames the parents for the child's condition. But this is an inaccurate perception of object relations therapy. We do not judge. We do want to help the family change behavior that is affecting symptomatology manifest in one of its members and to modify an individual's valency for expressing family-wide vulnerability. Reviewing their part in a pattern offers families this opportunity, while not placing the blame on any single family member.

DO YOU USE MEDICATION?

Medication is often required for major mental illnesses, serious breakdown, and psychiatric emergencies, such as suicide and psychosis, not immediately amenable to psychotherapy. The use of medication is adjunctive to object relations therapy, as with any psychotherapy. We are interested in the careful evaluation of the use of medication as a component of an integrated treatment.

Nevertheless, we do not rush to medicate, especially in outpatient treatment. We think that problems in living, relational problems, and depression and anxiety associated with conflictual matters are best dealt with by psychotherapy. Many more syndromes and symptoms are treatable by psychotherapy than is often thought. When in doubt, we would prefer to proceed with a course of intensive object relations psychotherapy in order to see if that alone is enough before we would recommend prescribing medicine, providing only that the patient's life and well-being are not in imminent danger.

IS OBJECT RELATIONS THERAPY HELPFUL IN MAJOR MENTAL ILLNESS, INCLUDING PSYCHOSIS?

It is fully compatible with the general approach to treating the psychotic patient. Although some early theoreticians thought that psychosis could be fully treated by the object relations approach, we now recognize that the biochemical imbalance in most of the major mental illnesses requires pharmacological support. Therapy is still relevant to those elements of character maladjustment, personality issues, secondary effects, and rehabilitation involving psychological growth of the individual. In these cases, we recommend psychotherapy in partnership with relevant medication, with psychoeducation, and with family therapy. The therapy might well have an ego-supportive quality, but it would still involve significant aspects of uncovering and reconstruction.

In the hospital treatment of major mental illness, object relations theory is helpful in understanding the dynamics found in hospital wards. Object relations theory applied to groups shows us how communities of in-patients will develop subgroups formed in the hope of meeting unconscious needs that have been frustrated in the context of the therapeutic relationship with the staff. Main, and Stanton and Schwartz have described how patterns of behavior occurring in the therapeutic community reflect each patient's intrapsychic dynamics.

DOES PROJECTIVE IDENTIFICATION OCCUR IN SEXUAL ABUSE?

The parent may view the child as a representative either of a part of the self that was abused by his or her parents or, alternatively, as that abusive parental object. In other words, the parent may treat the child as a part of the ego or the object. In actual behavior, then, the parent may both comfort and hurt the child. The child becomes an exciting sexualized object that is adored and hated. Introjective identification with the part of the self projected into the abused child then re-creates for the parent the trauma of the original abusive situation. In this way, projective and introjective identificatory mechanisms perpetuate the trauma of abuse through the generations.

IS THERE AN OBJECT RELATIONS APPROACH TO AFFAIRS?

We have written about this in our previous books on sexuality and on couple therapy. Affairs are seen as a splitting of aspects of the couple's intimate and sexual life and projection into an alternative relationship. An affair can be seen as an attempt to find through this other relationship a capacity for an exciting or creative sexual relationship that can be imported to revitalize the impoverished primary relationship. Affairs are an example of splitting and repression occurring in the interpersonal realm rather than the intrapsychic realm. When the split-off and repressed issues cannot be retrieved, the affair may become central and the present marriage ceases to be the primary relationship. For the couple therapist, the present marriage remains the primary focus. Elements split out into one or more affairs need to be understood as belonging to the primary marital relationship and reintegrated with the couple's shared marital issues if the marriage is to be helped.

An affair arises from a deficit in both the holding and centered relationships of the marriage. It represents issues that have been split off and, when the affair is kept secret, repressed outside the boundary of the couple relationship. So, understanding the cause of the affair is the first step toward reintegrating the split in the couple's marriage and the individual's capacity for intimate relating.

HOW DO YOU UNDERSTAND HOMOSEXUALITY?

Nowadays, homosexuality is not understood as pathological, but as one of the potential patterns for human sexual development and sexual object choice. As one of the outcomes in human development, it is, of course, influenced by the primary objects. The influence of the child's experience with both mother and father and the quality of their relationship is important. The parents present to the children a broad spectrum of internal objects, inclusive of their sexual aspects, for relating. These are relevant to the developmental pathways that include heterosexuality, homosexuality, and bisexuality.

Homosexuals may seek treatment for discomfort with their homosexual orientation or, more commonly, with other aspects of their life or relational abilities. If the treatment is intensive and thorough, it will, of course, involve exploration of early life experiences, including those that were formative in the development of gender and sexual object choice. This does not imply a bias as to the preferred outcome any more than when comparable exploration is conducted with a heterosexual patient.

To Understand the Perversions, Do You Need a Drive-Oriented Model?

The original psychoanalytic explanation of perversions — as for homosexuality, which was formerly regarded as a perversion — was built on a drive model. According to Sigmund Freud and Hans Sachs, perversions represent an isolated piece of childhood sexuality maintained through to adult development. Perverse sexuality was regarded as normal during early development. When pathways to mature oedipal development are blocked, the individual remains fixated at this stage.

These early explanations need broadening into a relational model. Nowadays, we see perversions as isolated and sexualized aspects of relating that have taken on a concrete, part-object, non-symbolic form and have been maintained as a compromise in the capacity of the patient to relate to whole objects with genitals. In object relations therapy we try to understand the specific difficulties in relating to objects that led to the need for this compromise.

OBJECT RELATIONS THEORY HOLDS THAT EXPERIENCE WITH BOTH MOTHER AND FATHER IS IMPORTANT, SO HOW CAN IT BE APPLIED TO WORK WITH A SINGLE-PARENT FAMILY?

Being a single parent is a handicapping condition. In handling the onslaught of developing children, the single parent is inevitably under more stress than a team of two parents, provided that the two parents get along reasonably well with each other and work together.

Each parent presents to the children his or her own internal couple, a psychic structure that mediates the capacity for important and intimate relationships. The internal couple is based on the person's experience of the parental couple relationship, modified by knowledge of other couples and by previous experience in adult intimate relationships. Thus, the single mother may present to her child her image of herself in relationship to a man, whether she is actually in a relationship to a man or not. The father does the same in terms of his relationship to a woman. It is not a single version of an internal couple that is presented but a wide range of possibilities. This happens in the ordinary course of events as a single parent talks about other couples, remembers her parents, or shares her hopes and fears for her child's development and capacity to relate. Thus, it is entirely possible for a single parent to present a full range of possibilities for the child's capacity to be in a loving and sexual relationship as an adult.

This is also possible if the parent is homosexual, although we wonder if the internal couple that such a homosexual parent presents would include a full range of possibilities for development or would be skewed more toward a homosexual couple, just as the heterosexual parents' internal couple will be skewed toward a heterosexual couple. Research, however, implies that homosexual couples may present the full range of options to their children. Homosexual couples also carry within them internal heterosexual couples based on their experience of the heterosexual couples who were their birth parents and usually also raised them.

IS OBJECT RELATIONS THERAPY APPLICABLE TO SUICIDAL EMERGENCIES?

If a patient's life is at risk, the capacity for trust and the risk of suicide have to be assessed, and appropriate plans for management of the risk situation have to be implemented immediately. Here, object relations therapy provides for a safe holding context within which the centered therapy relationship can form. If we can understand what contributes to the patient's suicidal ideation, we can begin to move the patient from danger to the self toward understanding the relational element in their depressive panic.

We view the suicidal impulse in the ways shown in Table 16–1.

Table 16–1. The Object Relations of Attempted Suicide
1. An attack on the internal object with which the self is identified
2. An attack on the self to spare the object
3. An attempt to separate the self from the object when they are hopelessly and destructively fused

Making the unconscious constellation conscious helps the patient to give up the suicidal ideation.

OBJECT RELATIONS THERAPY SOUNDS SO COMPLICATED. MUST IT TAKE A LONG TIME?

We tend to think of object relations therapy as a long-term method going on over years rather than months. It is, however, a way of working and thinking about clinical situations that can be quite helpful for short-term work.

HOW CAN IT HELP THOSE OF US IN MANAGED-CARE SITUATIONS?

In a health maintenance organization or managed-care situation, we do not have the luxury of taking as long as we would want. Some therapists adjust to the reality of the four-session contract by intervening more actively in the hope that if the therapist does more in the limited situation, the patient will get better faster. We have found that this does not bear out in practice. It is more useful to spend the time giving the patient a way of thinking and working with a psychodynamic approach that shows how much needs to be done and how it could be accomplished, rather than try to do a little desperately in too short a time. Time is better spent educating the patient in what can be done than in deluding him and the sponsoring agency into thinking that four sessions are going to be enough for any except basically healthy people in short-term developmental crises.

For instance, in the student mental health field, young patients face the anxiety of beginning school away from home, forming and breaking intimate and sexual relationships, roommate disputes, academic crises, and changes in their parents' situations. Married students may seek help for marital tension due to overwork or academic pressure, or for adjusting to the increased emotional and financial responsibilities of having a child.

Others may need help in adjusting to a physical illness. Here, a brief approach that focuses on the challenge that has temporarily overwhelmed the adaptational capacities of the individual or family often enables the individual or family to move back to its previous level of good adjustment within one to three sessions. If patients discover that there are longer-term issues underlying these crises, they can consider what kind of help they would need to attempt a more thorough readjustment. The patient and therapist together can consider alternate possibilities, including low-fee therapy outside the health maintenance organization or counseling center. This often enables the patient to decide to make the required economic and emotional investment, even when that investment will not be supported by the insuring institution.

IS INTENSIVE OBJECT RELATIONS THERAPY ONLY FOR THE RICH AND THE WELL-EDUCATED?

Of course, long-term therapy calls for a financial commitment. As more therapists are becoming trained in the object relations therapy method, more of the agencies that offer reduced-fee counseling are able to offer object relations therapy as part of their therapeutic armamentarium. Psychoanalytic institutes offer low fee psychoanalysis to motivated applicants who qualify for fee reduction. Object relations therapy is not only for the well-educated. The potential patient does require a degree of psychological-mindedness to communicate with the therapist in the language of object relations, but we have found that psychological-mindedness does not correlate directly with intelligence, level of education, or cultural background. There are some patients among the rich, the well-educated, and the privileged who are unable to work in an object relations method and require a more educational approach. Similarly, there are patients from disadvantaged communities, with limited language capacity or mental handicap, who work well on relationships and feelings and feel grateful for insight. They may welcome this new vista on understanding their lives and make more use of it than do some more sophisticated patients.

NOTES

This chapter gives an object relations bird's-eye view of various conditions such as alcoholism, addiction, suicide, anorexia, learning disorders, psychosis, and sexual perversion. We consider the object relations approach to homosexuality and affairs. We conclude with thoughts on the relevance of object relations theory to short-term therapy and managed care:

Intrapsychic and institutional dynamics (Main 1957, Stanton and Schwartz 1954).
Affairs (Scharff 1982, Scharff and Scharff 1991).
Perversion (Freud 1905, Joseph, 1989, Sachs 1923).
Psychosis (Kernberg 1975, Ogden 1982, Pao 1979, Searles 1965, Volkan 1987).
Anorexia (Ravenscroft 1988, Selvini Palazzoli 1974).

SEVENTEEN

The Role and Experience of the Object Relations Therapist

WHAT ARE YOUR VALUES AS OBJECT RELATIONS THERAPISTS?

We value insight, psychological-mindedness, and the importance of making the unconscious conscious by experiencing it in the countertransference and then revealing it to the patient in an interpretive mode. We value maturation and growth and the developmental process. We do not value symptom relief without in-depth reconstruction.

HOW DO YOU VIEW SYMPTOMS?

Symptomatology is seen as a compromise between unacceptable ways of relating and the demands of current relationships. Symptom removal is not the goal of object relations therapy. Therapy consists in making the unconscious conscious so as to recover lost, repressed parts of the self and make more of the self available for interaction with and modification by external objects.

HOW DO YOU ADDRESS THE PEOPLE WHO ARE IN THERAPY WITH YOU?

When we are working with people in consultation, we usually use surnames. In families, we call parents by their surnames and the children by their forenames. In couple therapy, we use surnames in the opening phase of therapy, but as we get to know the couple, who naturally are calling each other by their first names, we tend to use the more informal form of address within the session, although in communicating on the telephone we tend to revert to the more formal form of address. In individual therapy, we use surnames except with children, adolescents, and very young adults.

DOESN'T THE USE OF THE TERM PATIENTS GO AGAINST THE NONAUTHORITARIAN STANCE OF OBJECT RELATIONS THERAPY?

Not in our view. As physicians, we think of ourselves as working with patients. There is no pejorative connotation to us in the use of this terminology. It is simply analogous to social workers and counselors working with clients or teachers working with students. The likelihood of transfer of an authoritarian role relationship from earlier experience with physicians of the body needs to be considered and interpreted, but that does not negate the possibility of a collaborative stance. Personal respect and integrity transcend the boundaries of terminology.

HOW IS THE THERAPIST DIFFERENT IN THE EARLY, MIDDLE, AND LATE PHASES OF THERAPY?

The main distinguishing feature is the therapist's capacity to work with the patient. In the early phase, there is a greater tendency for the therapist to be as resistant as the patient is to uncovering anxiety-provoking material. This is not a devious or pathological collusion. Therapists are simply caught up in the defensive process. Unless they are affected in this way, they are unable to know what they and the patient have to work beyond. In the middle phase, we see that both therapist and patient have an increased capacity to analyze resistance and to move into areas of greater anxiety. In the late phases of therapy, we see a more collaborative, whole object relationship between therapist and patient with fewer, shorter-lived reversions to primitive relating to the therapist as a part-object.

HOW ARE OBJECT RELATIONS EXPERIENCED IN THERAPY?

The internal object relationships of the patient or patient group operate as a kind of map or script of relationships to be re-created with the therapist. These re-created relationships in therapy are re-editions of the original relationships to the objects of infantile dependency. A relatively conscious and mature or collaborative relationship that corresponds to the ideal or good enough object relationship enjoyed by the central ego governs the quality of the therapeutic alliance, which will be enlivened by or assaulted by the unconscious internal object relationship of the exciting or rejecting sort, respectively. As the therapist contains the expression of these repressed object relationships, the patient is enabled to modify and rework their more troublesome aspects.

CAN YOU GIVE AN EXAMPLE OF AN OBJECT RELATIONSHIP EXPERIENCED IN THERAPY?

Individual therapy

Mr. Donald would have preferred to see a male therapist, he told me (JSS). He did not like my office furnishings, the neighborhood of my home office, or my high fee. I should live where he did, charge the same fee per hour as he did, and redecorate my office in leather. He attacked my attempts to link his feelings about me to his history. I was left feeling rather destroyed and unable to think of what to say next, or remember what I had just said. It was as if I was not there. When I learned later of his relationship with his mother, I was able to see what he had been re-creating in the transference. She used to insist that he go shopping with her when he would rather have been playing soccer with his friends. He hated her habit of trying hats on *him* to see if they would suit *her* face. Like him as a child, I felt coerced, turned into the opposite sex, my autonomous, thinking self temporarily annihilated. He was giving me to feel as he had felt as a child in relation to his mother. I experienced a concordant countertransference, concordant with his self in relation to him as the annihilating maternal object. The repressed object relationship was re-created in the transference. There was also evidence of just enough central ego functioning in relation to me as a good enough object that he continued to attend his sessions, pay the fee promptly, and contribute to a therapeutic alliance sufficient to support the emergence of this and other repressed object relationships.

DO YOU ALWAYS HAVE COUNTERTRANSFERENCE?

Yes. Countertransference and transference are constantly operating. Most of the time, however, countertransference remains unconscious and is experienced simply as a feeling of being in tune with the patient. At moments, however, it obtrudes. The therapist becomes conscious of a countertransference response that is puzzling or jarring or in some way interferes with the unconscious automatic piloting mechanism that keeps the therapist in tune and on track. Attending to the countertransference creates a reflective space between the experiencing and observing parts of the therapist. Here the therapist finds room and time for process and review to figure out how experience in the here-and-now with the patient reflects the patient's unconscious object relations set.

HOW DO YOU KNOW THAT YOUR COUNTERTRANSFERENCE ISN'T "JUST YOU AND YOUR PROBLEMS"?

It is you. It is always you, but it has been stimulated in response to the patient. You want to check, however, that you do not always import a typical and repetitive countertransference based on your own neurotic conflicts. The only safeguard against this is to ensure that you have been adequately treated in your own personal therapy or psychoanalysis. You also subject your own reactions constantly to process and review. If you discover that the countertransference has been contributed to more by your own problems than by a feeling response in reaction to the patient, then it is best to simply admit it to yourself and work on it, rather than imposing it on the patient and insisting that the patient deal with an interpretation that you arrived at from a false basis. You will learn that your own areas of weakness can become the very places where you will be most acutely receptive to patients' transference difficulties. With knowledge, experience, and treatment, these areas of weakness can be turned into strengths.

IS PSYCHOTHERAPY FOR THE THERAPIST ALWAYS REQUIRED?

Few of us have the maturity to conduct reliable therapy without our own experience of therapy. Even when therapists are basically healthy, their work will acquire more depth if they have also had the experience of exploring their unconscious object relations from the patient's side of the therapeutic relationship. Object relations therapy calls for therapists to use their own internal responses as a set of clues as to what the patient brings to them. They cannot read the clues unless they are sure of the validity of their responses. The experience of themselves gathered in their personal therapy provides the baseline for knowing themselves well enough so that they can have confidence in knowing when something foreign to their internal reality has been experienced because of the encounter with the patient. We encourage all of our trainees to have a substantial experience of personal therapy or psychoanalysis, even when it is not necessary for their personal life.

WHEN WORKING WITH COUPLES AND FAMILIES, HOW DO YOU DECIDE TO WORK TOGETHER IN CO-THERAPY AND HOW DOES CO-THERAPY CHANGE YOUR WAY OF WORKING?

We tend not to work together in co-therapy. We find that we can usually do the work alone as well as with a co-therapist, and this is more economical. Sometimes, however, a family will be particularly difficult; for instance, when there is more than one hyperactive child, a co-therapist may be found necessary to support the holding environment. At other times, we choose to work in co-therapy for the opportunity of learning from a colleague and experiencing the transference within the co-therapy relationship rather than in the intrapsychic realm, as occurs when one is working alone.

Co-therapy changes the way of working by changing the focus of the countertransference. In co-therapy, the countertransference is experienced within the co-therapy relationship. We find ourselves dealing with our co-therapist according to a particular object relationship pattern that reflects a repressed object relationship operating between the couple or members of the family. This can usefully be demonstrated to the family or couple when the co-therapists talk about their experience and relate it to the family. When the co-therapists are married, as we are, the therapists' own marital issues are stirred by the task of allowing the transference to resonate in the co-therapy relationship. As a married co-therapy pair, we must agree to confront our own internal couple so that the couple in therapy can distinguish their internal couple that they have projected into us. This process and review tends to take longer and be more complicated than for the co-therapy team that is not married. So, for economy of time and money, and to save ourselves and our families from the upset of the intrusion of work into the family life space, we usually choose not to work in co-therapy.

EIGHTEEN

The Development of the Therapeutic Capacity

HOW CAN YOU BEAR TO WORK THIS CLOSELY WITH PEOPLE?

Ours is difficult work if we do it properly. It throws us into the farthest recesses of our own personalities, and it makes us confront parts of ourselves that we find problematic. We can bear the work only if we have sufficient support for doing it. By this we do not mean current support so much as resources built into ourselves. These resources come from previous clinical experience and from supervision, peer supervision, consultation, and therapy. We choose to be therapists because of our own internal object relations set: we need to repair objects that we feel our sadistic attachments have damaged. To some extent, then, it is gratifying to us to be somewhat hurt in our work life and to recover from it and to heal the parts of ourselves that we see in our patients. When, through therapy and continued clinical experience, we become healthier and have less need to make this kind of reparation, we can go through a period of boredom in our work. This is a moment where some therapists may quit or experience burnout. It is important to recognize that this is a phase in the growth and development of the therapist. We encourage therapists to seek help to get over this so as to be able to keep working, now from a new basis in healthier, more adaptive functioning, instead of from the previous masochistic position.

WHAT DOES WORK AS AN OBJECT RELATIONS THERAPIST DO TO YOU?

It can wear you down from time to time. It can get inside you, so that if you do not sufficiently metabolize your work, you may go home and start treating your family the way your patients have treated you. Sufficient time to process experiences is absolutely crucial and should take place in the office and not in the back-home setting. At the same time, object relations therapy affords work that constantly challenges you. It requires and facilitates your continued personal growth. The gratification of being a therapist lies in finding yourself gradually more capable of dealing with a wider range of problems. There is no danger of feeling, as a surgeon we knew once felt, that you have already done so many of the same kinds of procedures that there is nothing new anymore. The human personality is infinitely more subtle and demanding than the body. It requires greater agility, ingenuity, and capacity for tolerating ambiguity from which both patient and therapist can grow.

How Do You Take Care of Yourself so that You Can Do This Kind of Work?

Again, individual supervision and peer group supervision are essential, until the therapist feels able to work alone. Even then, the wise therapist will seek consultation for difficult situations in order to maximize effectiveness. Most therapists need an experience in personal therapy or psychoanalysis, even when this has not been necessary for them to enjoy their own life and love relations. Only in this way can they summon up more repressed aspects of their own personalities and press them into therapeutic service. The therapist must also actively develop an intimate and social life so that no patient or client bears the burden of being the therapist's major gratifying object. Otherwise, the therapist is too afraid of the abandoning object, which the patient will become as soon as the patient is well enough to leave the therapist, in which case improvement and progress may be seriously compromised.

When You Say Supervision, Do You Mean Through the One-Way Screen?

No. We do not use the one-way screen, because even though supervisors can see and hear what is being said and done, they cannot know the therapist's internal experience. Supervisors get to know the internal experience only by working with the self-report of the therapist and by monitoring the resonance of the therapist's experience of the patient within the supervisory relationship. The supervisor offers a psychological space to the therapist in which supervisor and therapist together can explore the therapist's

186

unconscious responses to the patient or patient group under discussion. Examples of the use of countertransference in supervision can be found in *Projective and Introjective Identification and the Use of the Therapist's Self* and in *Refinding the Object and Reclaiming the Self*.

HOW DO YOU COPE WITH TERMINATION?

You cope with termination by thinking of it from the first day. The end of every session presages termination. Attention to the end of the session deals with issues of separation and reminds a therapist and patient of the day when they will part. When the patient is ready to terminate, the therapist will go through a process of loss that runs parallel with that of the patient. Therapist and patient together will mourn the loss of the treatment opportunity, even while they together rejoice in its no longer being necessary.

A steady source of referrals is certainly a help.

HOW DO YOU DEAL WITH PATIENTS OR CLIENTS AFTER THERAPY IS COMPLETED?

We do not seek personal relationships with patients or clients after therapy. Nevertheless, we may meet former patients as new neighbors, parents at our children's schools or soccer games, party guests, and professional colleagues. In some of these situations, we may want to welcome a relationship on a new basis, but we remain sensitive to the influence of the previous therapeutic relationship. We know that former patients continue to think of us in terms of our therapeutic role and experience us as an internal presence integrated into their psychological structure, which, even if metabolized, exerts the influence of an internal object. Even the well-analyzed transference is potentially there, although no longer applicable, and the former therapist no longer has the authority to address its resurgence. The therapist who has not anticipated this revival of the transference may have to do some post-therapy self-analysis to accommodate to the role shift without the usual tool of interpretation.

Under no circumstances do we want to have intimate, sexual relationships with current or former clients, including those who become our colleagues or students. Our influence is such that we can never be sure that there is not a transference relationship determining the nature of their interest in us. If we feel drawn to make an exception, we need to reexamine our countertransference to the patient and to the termination. It is preferable that we seek our intimate, social, and sexual relationships among the many people who have not consulted with us professionally.

This does not mean that we refuse to speak to former patients or clients. If we meet in a situation of professional colleagueship or social acquaintanceship, we want to behave naturally and unobtrusively with them, always following their needs. We do not allow our own longing, curiosity, or any remaining discomfort to lead us into seductive, rejecting, or impersonal behavior that is hurtful.

In agreeing to a contract for offering therapy and in accepting payment for our services, we make a commitment to subordinate our own interests in order to be the necessary therapeutic object for the patient. Our investment in the therapeutic process is our compensation for the personal loss that we must take for the patient's sake.

IV

The Object Relations Therapist: Further Training and Guided Reading

NINETEEN

A Guide to Further Reading

The introductory readings that we are about to recommend are fully referenced in the reference section that follows. Here, we want to tell you briefly what we have found most helpful.

We suggest starting with Ronald Fairbairn's *Psychoanalytic Studies of the Personality,* Hanna Segal's *Introduction to the Work of Melanie Klein,* and Donald Winnicott's simple book, *The Child, the Family and the Outside World.* All these books are quite accessible and readable. Segal's and Fairbairn's texts are focused on object relations theory whereas Winnicott's is a good overview of his approach to development and family life. A short, simple volume called *Love, Hate and Reparation* by

Melanie Klein and Joan Riviere puts Kleinian theory into everyday language.

The most succinct introduction to Klein and Fairbairn can be found in David Scharff's *The Sexual Relationship: An Object Relations View of Sex and the Family,* Appendix A. An expanded simple introduction to the British object relations theorists is in David and Jill Scharff's *Object Relations Family Therapy,* Chapters 3 and 4. An excellent concise overview is given in Jock Sutherland's article, "The British Object Relations Theorists: Balint, Winnicott, Fairbairn, Guntrip." A good summary of the major contributions to object relations theory is included in Judith Hughes's book, *Reshaping the Psychoanalytic Domain: The Work of Melanie Klein, W. R. D. Fairbairn and D. W. Winnicott.* We also recommend N. Gregory Hamilton's basic text *Self and Others.*

FAIRBAIRN TO READ

Fairbairn's papers are collected in his book, *Psychoanalytic Studies of the Personality.* His paper "On the Nature of Hysterical States," written later than the book and published in the *British Journal of Medical Psychology,* is so interesting that it is worth the trouble of trying to find it. For a quick guide, look at Fairbairn's one-page "Synopsis of an Object Relations Theory of the Personality" in *The International Journal of Psycho-Analysis.* Fairbairn's ideas are modified to include the regressed ego in Harry Guntrip's *Schizoid Phenomena, Object Relations and the Self,* of which pages 288–331 are particularly helpful in clinical practice.

FURTHER READING ON WINNICOTT'S CONCEPTS

A readable account of the development of Winnicott's ideas in their philosophical context is to be found in Adam Phillips's *Winnicott,* a small, scholarly volume that does justice to the complexity and ambiguity of Winnicott's whimsical theorizing. A useful, less complicated statement of the concepts appears in Simon Grolnick's *The Work and Play of Winnicott.* Turning to the original, Winnicott's work is spread through many papers that are collected in two volumes called *Collected Papers* and *The Maturational Process and the Facilitating Environment,* both of which you might enjoy dipping into. A more advanced, better-integrated collection of Winnicott's ideas appears in *Playing and Reality,* his last major book before his death.

MORE READING ABOUT KLEINIAN CONCEPTS

Melanie Klein's discursive writing style can be difficult for the student reader, who will get a better grasp of the concepts from reading Segal. If you are interested in reading the original, we suggest that you start with "Notes on Some Schizoid Mechanisms" in *Envy and Gratitude and Other Works* and "A Contribution to the Psychogenesis of Manic-depressive States" in *Love, Guilt and Reparation.* The Kleinian concepts of projective and introjective identification are explored and summarized in Jill Savege Scharff's book *Projective and Introjective Identification and the Use of the Therapist's Self,* Chapters 2, 3, and 4.

Like Klein's, Wilfred Bion's work is fascinating for the advanced reader, but it is extremely difficult to understand in the original. If you are ready for the challenge, begin with *Learning from Experience.* Fortunately his ideas on groups, knowledge, psychosis, thought, transformations, and psychoanalytic practice have been simplified and summarized by León Grinberg and some of Bion's other students in a little book called *Introduction to the Work of Bion.* His group theory is presented in Margaret Rioch's excellent exposition in *Psychiatry.*

APPLICATION TO COUPLE AND FAMILY THERAPY

British object relations theory is applied to marital dynamics in Henry Dicks's classic, *Marital Tensions;* to couple and family therapy in David and Jill Scharff's books, *Object Relations Family Therapy* and *Object Relations Couple Therapy;* and to sexuality in David Scharff's *The Sexual Relationship.* Original papers by Roger Shapiro and John Zinner, who applied object relations theory in their pioneering family research, appear in Jill Scharff's *Foundations of Object Relations Family Therapy.*

The interrelation of intrapsychic and interpersonal forces at work on the development of the self as it relates to its objects is explored in David Scharff's *Refinding the Object and Reclaiming the Self* and in an advanced text, *Object Relations Individual Therapy* by Jill Savege Scharff and David E. Scharff in preparation.

All of the above-mentioned books are fully cited in the References under the headings "Object Relations Theory" and "Application of Object Relations Theory to Couple and Family Therapy."

MORE ADVANCED READING

The advanced reader who is already familiar with the basics and wants to make a broader or deeper study of object relations theory and related psychoanalytic subjects may choose readings from the following annotated reference section. Of the various relevant contributions, we have found most useful the writings of Christopher Bollas, Patrick Casement, Nina Coltart, Betty Joseph, Stephen Mitchell, Thomas Ogden, Harold Searles, Hanna Segal, and books edited by Elizabeth Spillius. To guide you to your particular area of interest, we have grouped the references in nine categories: object relations theory of individual and group, application of object relations theory to couple and family therapy, integration of object relations theory with other approaches, American object relations theory, advanced integration of British object relations theory and the American interpersonalists with classical Freudian theory, countertransference, self psychology, Freudian theory, and other relevant contributions.

References

OBJECT RELATIONS THEORY OF INDIVIDUAL AND GROUP

Anderson, R., ed. (1992). *Clinical Lectures of Klein and Bion.* Number 14 in The New Library of Psychoanalysis. London: Routledge and Kegan Paul.

Balint, M. (1968). *The Basic Fault.* London: Tavistock.

Bick, E. (1968). The experience of the skin in early object relations. *International Journal of Psycho-Analysis* 49:484–486.

———— (1986). Further considerations on the role of the skin in early object relations. *British Journal of Psychotherapy* 2:292–299.

Bion, W. R. (1959). *Experiences in Groups.* New York: Basic Books, 1961.

———— (1962). *Learning from Experience.* New York: Basic Books.

———— (1967). *Second Thoughts.* London: Heinemann. (Reprinted Karnac 1984.)

Bollas, C. (1987). *The Shadow of the Object.* New York: Columbia University Press.

_____ (1989a). A theory for the true self. In *Forces of Destiny: Psychoanalysis and Human Idiom*. London: Free Association Books.

_____ (1989b). *Forces of Destiny: Psychoanalysis and Human Idiom*. London: Free Association Books.

_____ (1992). *Being a Character*. New York: Faber and Faber.

Bowlby, J. (1969). *Attachment and Loss*. Vol. 1: *Attachment*. New York: Basic Books.

_____ (1973). *Attachment and Loss*. Vol. 2: *Separation: Anxiety and Anger*. New York: Basic Books.

_____ (1980). *Attachment and Loss* Vol. 3: *Loss: Sadness and Depression*. New York: Basic Books.

Casement, P. (1991). *On Learning from the Patient*. New York: Guilford Press.

Coltart, N. (1992). *Slouching Towards Bethlehem*. New York: Guilford Press.

Dicks, H. V. (1967). *Marital Tensions: Clinical Studies Towards a Psychoanalytic Theory of Interaction*. London: Routledge and Kegan Paul.

Fairbairn, W. R. D. (1944). Endopsychic structure considered in terms of object relationships. In *Psychoanalytic Studies of the Personality*, pp. 82–135. London: Routledge and Kegan Paul, 1952.

_____ (1952). *Psychoanalytic Studies of the Personality*. London: Routledge and Kegan Paul. (Also published as *An Object Relations Theory of the Personality*. New York: Basic Books.)

_____ (1954). Observations on the nature of hysterical states. *British Journal of Medical Psychology* 27:105–125.

_____ (1958). On the nature and aims of psycho-analytical treatment. *International Journal of Psycho-Analysis* 39:374–385.

_____ (1963). Synopsis of an object-relations theory of the personality. *International Journal of Psycho-Analysis* 44:224–225.

Greenberg, J. R., and Mitchell, S. A. (1983). *Object Relations in Psychoanalytic Theory*. Cambridge, MA: Harvard University Press.

Grinberg, L., Sor, D., and Tabak de Bianchedi, E. (1975). *Introduction to the Work of Bion*. Trans. A. Hahn. Strath Tay, Scotland: Clunie Press.

Grolnick, S. (1990). *The Work and Play of Winnicott*. Northvale, NJ: Jason Aronson.

Guntrip, H. (1961). *Personality Structure and Human Interaction: The Developing Synthesis of Psychodynamic Theory*. London: Hogarth Press and The Institute of Psycho-Analysis.

_____ (1969). *Schizoid Phenomena, Object Relations and the Self*. New York: International Universities Press.

_____ (1986). My experience of analysis with Fairbairn and Winnicott. In *Essential Papers on Object Relations*, ed. P. Buckley, pp. 447–468. New York: New York University Press.

Heimann, P. (1950). On counter-transference. *International Journal of Psycho-Analysis* 31:81–84.

Hamilton, N. G. (1988). *Self and Others: Object Relations Theory in Practice*. Northvale, NJ: Jason Aronson.

Hinshelwood, R. D. (1991). *A Dictionary of Kleinian Thought*. Northvale, NJ:

Jason Aronson.

Hughes, J. M. (1989). *Reshaping the Psychoanalytic Domain: The Work of Melanie Klein, W. R. D. Fairbairn & D. W. Winnicott.* Berkeley: University of California Press.

Joseph, B. (1989). *Psychic Equilibrium and Psychic Change: Selected Papers of Betty Joseph.* Ed. M. Feldman and E. B. Spillius. Number 9 in The New Library of Psychoanalysis. London: Tavistock/Routledge.

Klein, M. (1935). A contribution to the psychogenesis of manic-depressive states. In *Love, Guilt and Reparation and Other Works 1921-1945,* pp. 262–289. London: Hogarth Press, 1975.

———— (1946). Notes on some schizoid mechanisms. *International Journal of Psycho-Analysis* 27:99–100. And in *Envy and Gratitude & Other Works, 1946-1963.* London: Hogarth Press and the Institute of Psycho-Analysis, 1975.

———— (1948). *Contributions to Psycho-Analysis 1921-1945.* London: Hogarth Press.

———— (1952). Some theoretical conclusions regarding the emotional life of the infant. In *Envy and Gratitude and Other Works 1946-1963,* pp. 61–93. London: Hogarth Press and The Institute of Psycho-Analysis, 1975.

———— (1955). On identification. In *Envy and Gratitude and Other Works 1946-1963,* pp. 141–175. London: Hogarth Press and The Institute of Psycho-Analysis, 1975.

———— (1957). *Envy and Gratitude and Other Works 1946-1963.* London: Hogarth Press and The Institute of Psycho-Analysis, 1975.

———— (1975). *Love, Guilt and Reparation and Other Works 1921-1945.* London: Hogarth Press.

Klein, M., and Riviere, J. (1967). *Love, Hate and Reparation.* London: The Hogarth Press and The Institute of Psycho-Analysis.

Little, M. (1951). Counter-transference and the patient's response to it. *International Journal of Psycho-Analysis* 32:32–39.

Main, T. F. (1957). The ailment. *British Journal of Medical Psychology* 30:129–145.

Meltzer, D. (1975). Adhesive identification. *Contemporary Psychoanalysis* 11:289–310.

Mitchell, S. A. (1988). *Relational Concepts in Psychoanalysis: An Integration.* Cambridge, MA: Harvard University Press.

Money-Kyrle, R. (1956). Normal counter-transference and some of its deviations. *International Journal of Psycho-Analysis* 37:360–366.

Murray, J. M. (1955). *Keats.* New York: Noonday Press.

Ogden, T. H. (1982). *Projective Identification and Psychotherapeutic Technique.* New York: Jason Aronson.

———— (1986a). Internal object relations. Chapter 6 in *The Matrix of the Mind,* pp. 131–165. Northvale, NJ: Jason Aronson.

———— (1986b). *The Matrix of the Mind.* Northvale, NJ: Jason Aronson.

———— (1989a). The autistic-contiguous position. In *The Primitive Edge of Experience,* pp. 47–81. Northvale, NJ: Jason Aronson.

200

_____ (1989b). *The Primitive Edge of Experience*. Northvale, NJ: Jason Aronson.

Phillips, A. (1988). *Winnicott*. Cambridge, MA: Harvard University Press.

Racker, H. (1968). *Transference and Countertransference*. New York: International Universities Press.

Rioch, M. (1970). The work of Wilfred Bion on groups. *Psychiatry* 33: 56–65.

Sandler, J., ed. (1987). *Projection, Identification and Projective Identification*. Madison, CT: International Universities Press.

Scharff, D. E. (1982). *The Sexual Relationship: An Object Relations View of Sex and the Family*. London: Routledge and Kegan Paul.

_____ (1992). *Refinding the Object and Reclaiming the Self*. Northvale, NJ: Jason Aronson.

Scharff, D. E., and Scharff, J. S. (in preparation). *Object Relations Individual Therapy*. Northvale, NJ: Jason Aronson.

Scharff, J. S. (1992). *Projective and Introjective Identification and the Use of the Therapist's Self*. Northvale, NJ: Jason Aronson.

Searles, H. (1965). *Collected Papers on Schizophrenia and Related Subjects*. New York: International Universities Press.

_____ (1979). *Countertransference and Related Subjects — Selected Papers*. New York: International Universities Press.

_____ (1986). *My Work with Borderline Patients*. Northvale, NJ: Jason Aronson.

Segal, H. (1964). *Introduction to the Work of Melanie Klein*. London: Heinemann.

_____ (1981). *The Work of Hanna Segal*. New York: Jason Aronson.

_____ (1991). *Dream, Phantasy and Art*. Ed. E. B. Spillius. Number 12 in The New Library of Psychoanalysis. London: Routledge and Kegan Paul.

Spillius, E. (1992). Clinical experiences of projective identification. In *Clinical Lectures on Klein and Bion*. Ed. R. Anderson. Number 14 in The New Library of Psychoanalysis, pp. 59–73. London: Routledge and Kegan Paul.

_____ (1988a). *Melanie Klein Today. Volume 1: Mainly Theory*. Ed. E. B. Spillius. Number 7 in The New Library of Psychoanalysis. London and New York: Routledge and Kegan Paul.

_____ (1988b). *Melanie Klein Today. Volume 2: Mainly Practice*. Ed. E. B. Spillius. Number 8 in The New Library of Psychoanalysis. London: Routledge and Kegan Paul.

Stewart, H. (1990). Interpretation and other agents for psychic change. *International Review of Psycho-Analysis* 17:61–69.

_____ (1992). *Psychic Experience and Problems of Technique*. Number 13 in The New Library of Psychoanalysis. London and New York: Routledge.

Sutherland, J. (1963). Object relations theory and the conceptual model of psychoanalysis. *British Journal of Medical Psychology* 36:109–124.

_____ (1980). The British object relations theorists: Balint, Winnicott, Fairbairn, Guntrip. *Journal of the American Psychoanalytic Association* 28:829–860.

_____ (1989). *Fairbairn's Journey into the Interior*. London: Free Association Press.

Tustin, F. (1981). *Autistic States in Children*. Boston: Routledge and Kegan Paul.

_____ (1984). Autistic shapes. *International Review of Psycho-Analysis* 11:279–290.

_____ (1986). *Autistic Barriers in Neurotic Patients*. New Haven: Yale University Press.

Winnicott, D. W. (1945). Primitive emotional development. In *Through Paediatrics to Psycho-Analysis,* pp. 145–156. London: Hogarth Press, 1975.

_____ (1951). Transitional objects and transitional phenomena. In *Through Paediatrics to Psycho-Analysis,* pp. 229–242. London: Tavistock, 1958. (Reprinted by Hogarth Press, 1975.)

_____ (1956). Primary maternal preoccupation. In *Through Paediatrics to Psycho-Analysis,* pp. 300–305. London: Hogarth Press, 1965.

_____ (1958). *Through Paediatrics to Psycho-Analysis*. London: Tavistock, 1958. (Reprinted by Hogarth Press, 1975.)

_____ (1960). The theory of the parent–infant relationship. In *The Maturational Processes and the Facilitating Environment,* pp. 37–55. London: Hogarth Press, 1975.

_____ (1963a). Communicating and not communicating leading to a study of certain opposites. In *The Maturational Processes and the Facilitating Environment,* pp. 179–192. London: Hogarth Press, 1975.

_____ (1963b). The development of the capacity for concern. In *The Maturational Processes and the Facilitating Environment,* pp. 73–81. London: Hogarth Press, 1975.

_____ (1964). *The Child, the Family and the Outside World*. London: Penguin Books.

_____ (1965). *The Maturational Processes and the Facilitating Environment*. London: Hogarth Press.

_____ (1971). *Playing and Reality*. London: Tavistock.

APPLICATION OF OBJECT RELATIONS THEORY TO COUPLE AND FAMILY THERAPY

Box, S. (1981). Introduction: space for thinking in families. In *Psychotherapy with Families,* ed. S. Box et al., pp. 1–8. London: Routledge and Kegan Paul.

Box, S., Copley, B., Magagna, J., and Moustaki, E., eds. (1981). *Psychotherapy with Families: An Analytic Approach*. London: Routledge and Kegan Paul.

202

Dicks, H. V. (1967). *Marital Tensions: Clinical Studies Towards a Psychoanalytic Theory of Interaction.* London: Routledge and Kegan Paul.

Framo, J. L. (1970). Symptoms from a family transactional point of view. In *Family Therapy in Transition,* ed. N. Ackerman, J. Lieb, and J. Pearce, pp. 12–57. Boston: Little Brown.

Klein, R. S. (1990). *Object Relations and the Family Process.* New York: Praeger.

Luepnitz, D. (1988). Psychoanalytic theory as a conceptual source for feminist psychotherapy with families. Chapter 12 in *The Family Interpreted: Feminist Theory in Clinical Practice,* pp. 168–195. New York: Basic Books.

Main, T. F. (1966). Mutual projection in a marriage. *Comprehensive Psychiatry* 7:432–449.

McCormack, C. (in press). *The Borderline Marriage.* Northvale, NJ: Jason Aronson.

Ravenscroft, K. (1988). *Psychoanalytic family therapy approaches to the adolescent bulaemic.* In *Psychoanalytic Treatment and Theory,* ed. H. Schwartz, pp. 443–488. Madison, CT: International Universities Press.

Scharff, D. (1992). *Refinding the Object and Reclaiming the Self.* Northvale, NJ: Jason Aronson.

Scharff, D., and Scharff, J. S., (1987). *Object Relations Family Therapy,* Northvale, NJ: Jason Aronson.

———— (1991). *Object Relations Couple Therapy.* Northvale, NJ: Jason Aronson.

Scharff, J. S. (1989a). Play: an aspect of the therapist's holding capacity. In *Foundations of Object Relations Family Therapy,* pp. 447–461. Northvale, NJ: Jason Aronson.

————, ed. (1989b). *Foundations of Object Relations Family Therapy.* Northvale, NJ: Jason Aronson.

———— (1992). *Projective and Introjective Identification and the Use of the Therapist's Self.* Northvale, NJ: Jason Aronson.

Shapiro, R. L. (1979). Family dynamics and object relations theory: an analytic group-interpretive approach to family therapy. In *Foundations of Object Relations Family Therapy,* ed. J. S. Scharff, pp. 225–258. Northvale, NJ: Jason Aronson.

Stierlin, H. (1977). *Psychoanalysis and Family Therapy.* New York: Jason Aronson.

Williams, A. H. (1981). The micro-environment. In *Psychotherapy with Families,* ed. S. Box et al. pp. 105–119. London: Routledge and Kegan Paul.

Winer, R. (1989). The role of transitional experience in development in healthy and incestuous families. In *Foundations of Object Relations Family Therapy,* ed. J. S. Scharff, pp. 357–384. Northvale, NJ: Jason Aronson.

Zinner, J. (1989). The implications of projective identification for marital interaction. In *Foundations of Object Relations Family Therapy,* ed. J. Scharff, pp. 155–173. Northvale, NJ: Jason Aronson, 1976.

Zinner, J., and Shapiro, R. (1972). Projective identification as a mode of perception and behavior in families of adolescents. *International Journal of Psycho-Analysis* 53:523–530. Also in *Foundations of Object Relations Family Therapy,* ed. J. S. Scharff, pp. 109–126. Northvale, NJ: Jason Aronson.

———— (1985). The use of concurrent therapies: therapeutic strategy or re-enactment? In *Foundations of Object Relations Family Therapy,* ed. J. S. Scharff, pp. 321–333. Northvale, NJ: Jason Aronson.

INTEGRATION OF OBJECT RELATIONS THEORY WITH OTHER APPROACHES

Bacall, H. A., and Newman, K. M. (1990). *Theories of Object Relations: Bridges to Self Psychology.* New York: Columbia University Press.

Framo, J. L. (1992). *Family-of-Origin Therapy: An Intergenerational Approach.* New York: Brunner/Mazel.

Slipp, S. (1984). *Object Relations: A Dynamic Bridge Between Individual and Family Treatment.* New York: Jason Aronson.

———— (1988). *Theory and Practice of Object Relations Family Therapy.* Northvale, NJ: Jason Aronson.

St. Clair, M. (1986). *Object Relations and Self Psychology: An Introduction.* Monterey, CA: Brooks/Cole.

AMERICAN OBJECT RELATIONS THEORY

Grotstein, J. (1982). *Splitting and Projective Identification.* New York: Jason Aronson.

Jacobson, E. (1954). The self and the object world: vicissitudes of their infantile cathexes and their influence on ideational and affective development. *Psychoanalytic Study of the Child* 9:75–127. New York: International Universities Press.

———— (1965). *The Self and the Object World.* London: Hogarth Press.

Kernberg, O. F. (1975). *Borderline Conditions and Pathological Narcissism.* New York: Jason Aronson.

———— (1976). *Object Relations and Clinical Psychoanalysis.* New York: Jason Aronson.

_____ (1980). *Internal World and External Reality*. New York: Jason Aronson.

_____ (1987). Projection and projective identification: developmental and clinical aspects. In *Projection, Identification, Projective Identification,* ed. J. Sandler, pp. 93–115. Madison, CT: International Universities Press.

_____ (1991). Aggression and love in the relationship of the couple. *Journal of the American Psychoanalytic Association* 39:45–70.

Mahler, M. (1968). *On Human Symbiosis and the Vicissitudes of Individuation*. New York: International Universities Press.

Mahler, M., Pine, F., and Bergman, A. (1975). *The Psychological Birth of the Human Infant: Symbiosis and Individuation*. New York: Basic Books.

Masterson, J. (1981). *The Narcissistic and Borderline Disorders: An Integrated Developmental Approach*. New York: Brunner/Mazel.

Meissner, W. W. (1987). Projection and projective identification. In *Projection, Identification, Projective Identification,* ed. J. Sandler, pp. 27–49. Madison, CT: International Universities Press.

Rinsley, D. (1982). *Borderline and Other Self Disorders*. New York: Jason Aronson.

Sandler, J. (1987a). Projection and projective identification. In *Projection, Identification, Projective Identification,* pp. 93–115. Madison, CT: International Universities Press.

_____ (1987b). *Projection, Identification, Projective Identification*. Madison, CT: International Universities Press.

Siegel, J. (in press). *Repairing Intimacy: An Object Relations Approach to Couples Therapy*. Northvale, NJ: Jason Aronson.

Volkan, V. (1976). *Primitive Internalized Object Relations*. New York: International Universities Press.

_____ (1987). *Six Steps in the Treatment of Borderline Personality Organization*. Northvale, NJ: Jason Aronson.

Integrating British Object Relations and the American Interpersonalists with Classical Freudian Theory

Greenberg, J. R., and Mitchell, S. A. (1983). *Object Relations in Psychoanalytic Theory*. Cambridge, MA: Harvard University Press.

Mitchell, S. A. (1988). *Relational Concepts in Psychoanalysis: An Integration*. Cambridge, MA: Harvard University Press.

COUNTERTRANSFERENCE

Heimann, P. (1950). On counter-transference. *International Journal of Psycho-Analysis* 31:81–84.

Jacobs, T. J. (1991). *The Use of the Self.* Madison, CT: International Universities Press.

Racker, H. (1968). *Transference and Countertransference.* New York: International Universities Press.

Searles, H. (1979). *Countertransference and Related Subjects: Selected Papers.* New York: International Universities Press.

_____ (1986). *My Work with Borderline Patients.* Northvale, NJ: Jason Aronson.

SELF PSYCHOLOGY THEORY APPLIED TO INDIVIDUALS AND COUPLES

Kohut, H. (1971). *The Analysis of the Self.* New York: International Universities Press.

_____ (1977). *The Restoration of the Self.* New York: International Universities Press.

_____ (1982). Introspection, empathy, and the semi-circle of mental health. *International Journal of Psycho-Analysis* 63:395–407.

Lansky, M. (1981). Treatment of the narcissistically vulnerable marriage. In *Family Therapy and Major Psychopathology,* pp. 163–182. New York: Grune and Stratton.

Solomon, M. (1989). *Narcissism and Intimacy.* New York: Norton.

FREUDIAN THEORY

Freud, A. (1946). The ego's defensive operations. In *The Ego and the Mechanisms of Defense,* pp. 30–70. New York: International Universities Press.

Freud, S. (1895). The psychotherapy of hysteria. *Standard Edition* 2:253–305.

_____ (1900). The interpretation of dreams. *Standard Edition* 4:150–151.

_____ (1901a). The psychopathology of everyday life. *Standard Edition* 6:53–105.

_____ (1901b). On dreams. *Standard Edition* 5:633–686.

_____ (1905a). Fragment of an analysis of a case of hysteria. *Standard Edition* 7:7–122.

_____ (1905b). Three essays on the theory of sexuality. *Standard Edition* 7:135–243.

_____ (1910a). The future prospects of psycho-analytic therapy. Five lectures on psychoanalysis. *Standard Edition* 11:141–151.

_____ (1910b). A special type of object choice made by men. *Standard Edition* 11:165–175.

_____ (1911). Formulations on the two principles of mental functioning. *Standard Edition* 12:213–226.

_____ (1912). Recommendations to physicians practising psychoanalysis. *Standard Edition* 12:111–120.

_____ (1914). Remembering, repeating and working through. *Standard Edition* 12:147–156.

_____ (1915a). Repression. *Standard Edition* 14:146–158.

_____ (1915b). Observations on transference love. *Standard Edition* 12:159–171.

_____ (1915c). The unconscious. *Standard Edition* 14:166–204.

_____ (1917a). Mourning and melancholia. *Standard Edition* 14:243–258.

_____ (1917b). Transference. *Standard Edition* 16:431–447.

_____ (1917c). Resistance and repression. *Standard Edition* 16:286–302.

_____ (1920). Beyond the pleasure principle. *Standard Edition* 18:7–64.

_____ (1921). Group psychology and the analysis of the ego. *Standard Edition* 18:67–143.

_____ (1923). The ego and the id. *Standard Edition* 19:12–66.

_____ (1924). The dissolution of the Oedipus complex. *Standard Edition* 19:173–179.

_____ (1930). Civilization and its discontents. *Standard Edition* 21:64–145.

_____ (1933). New introductory lectures on psycho-analysis. *Standard Edition* 22:3–182.

_____ (1940). An outline of psychoanalysis. *Standard Edition* 23:144–207.

OTHER RELEVANT CONTRIBUTIONS

Chodorow, N. (1978). *The Reproduction of Mothering*. Berkeley: University of California Press.

Dare, C. (1986). Psychoanalytic marital therapy. In *Clinical Handbook of Marital Therapy,* ed. N. S. Jacobson and A. S. Gurman, pp. 13–28. New York: Guilford Press.

Erikson, E. (1950). The eight ages of man. In *Childhood and Society,* pp. 247–274. New York: Norton. Revised paperback edition 1963.

Foulkes, S. H. (1948). *Introduction to Group-Analytic Psychotherapy: Studies in the Social Integration of Individuals and Groups.* London: Heinemann. Reprinted London: Maresfield Reprints, 1983.

Gilligan, C. (1982). *In a Different Voice: Psychological Theory and Women's Development.* Cambridge: Harvard University Press.

Kaplan, H. S. (1974). *The New Sex Therapy: Active Treatment of Sexual Dysfunctions.* New York: Brunner/Mazel.

Langs, R. (1976). *The Therapeutic Interaction, Vol. 2: A Critical Overview and Synthesis.* New York: Jason Aronson.

Masters, W. H., and Johnson, V. E. (1970). *Human Sexual Inadequacy.* Boston: Little, Brown.

Miller, J. B. (1991). The development of women's sense of self. In *Women's Growth in Connection: Writings from the Stone Center,* pp. 11–26. New York: Guilford.

Pao, P.-N. (1979). *Schizophrenic Disorders.* New York: International Universities Press.

Selvini Palazzoli, M. (1974). *Self Starvation: From the Intrapsychic to the Transpersonal Approach to Anorexia Nervosa.* Trans. A. Pomerans. Milan: Feltrini. London: Human Context Books, Chaucer Publishing.

Stanton, A. H., and Schwartz, M. S. (1954). *The Mental Hospital: A Study of Institutional Participation in Psychiatric Illness and Treatment.* New York: Basic Books.

Stern, D. (1985). *The Interpersonal World of the Human Infant.* New York: Basic Books.

Strachey, J. (1934). The nature of the therapeutic action of psycho-analysis. *International Journal of Psycho-Analysis* 15:127–159.

Index

ABOUT THE AUTHORS

David E. Scharff, M.D., is Co-Director of the International Institute of Object Relations Therapy and Clinical Professor of Psychiatry at Georgetown and the Uniformed Services Universities. Dr. Scharff received his M.D. from Harvard and is board certified in adult and child psychiatry and certified in psychoanalysis by the American Psychoanalytic Association. He is a former President of the American Association of Sex Educators, Counselors, and Therapists.

Jill Savege Scharff, M.D., is Co-Director of the International Institute of Object Relations Therapy and Clinical Professor of Psychiatry at Georgetown University. Educated in Scotland, she moved to England for further training at the Tavistock Clinic and received membership in the Royal College of Psychiatrists before coming to the United States. Dr. Jill Scharff is board certified in adult and child psychiatry and certified in child and adult psychoanalysis by the American Psychoanalytic Association.

The Scharffs have a national and international reputation as authors, editors, teachers, and therapists. Among their publications are *Object Relations Family Therapy, Object Relations Couple Therapy, The Sexual Relationship, Foundations of Object Relations Family Therapy, Projective and Introjective Identification and the Use of the Therapist's Self, Refinding the Object and Reclaiming the Self, The Autonomous Self: The Work of John D. Sutherland, From Instinct to Self: The Selected Papers of W.R.D. Fairbairn, Object Relations Theory and Practice,* and the forthcoming *Fairbairn: Then and Now* and *Object Relations Individual Therapy.*